D0396585

The MONOCLE
Travel Guide Series

26

San Francisco

For more information, please visit *gestalten.com*

———

Bibliographic information published by the Deutsche Nationalbibliothek: The Deutsche Nationalbibliothek lists this publication in the Deutsche Nationalbibliografie; detailed bibliographic data are available online at *dnb.d-nb.de*

MIX
Paper from responsible sources
FSC
www.fsc.org
FSC® C011712

Monocle editor in chief and chairman:
Tyler Brûlé
Monocle editor: *Andrew Tuck*
Books editor: *Joe Pickard*
Guide editors: *Ed Stocker, Mikaela Aitken*

———

Designed by *Monocle*
Proofreading by *Monocle*
Typeset in *Plantin & Helvetica*

———

Printed by *Offsetdruckerei Grammlich, Pliezhausen*

Made in Germany

Published by *Gestalten*, Berlin 2017
ISBN 978-3-89955-921-7

© Die Gestalten Verlag GmbH & Co. KG, Berlin 2017

Welcome
—— Happy daze

OK, so you've heard of the *Beats* and *hippie culture*. And, yes, you're familiar with the Golden Gate Bridge and that thrilling James Bond fight scene (and a host of other film references, for that matter). Well, just you wait. You'll soon discover how many sides to this city there really are.

Despite its diminutive size, San Francisco packs it in. First, there's the implausible topography (vistas galore and the odd hairpin bend) and the equally erratic climate, with its cool breeze, flashes of *Californian sunshine* and *unpredictable fog*. Add to the mix the ridiculous bounty of natural beauty – from the Presidio and Golden Gate Park to the rocky coastline and grassy headlands just outside town – and you have a heady mix. And talking of heads (sore ones), let's not forget the *plentiful wine*, courtesy of nearby Napa and Sonoma.

Take a stroll and you'll quickly get a sense of the history of a town that rose to prominence during the Gold Rush. Ornate Victorian houses point to that boom, while the *lofty environs* of Nob Hill whisper old money. The city has continued to evolve, positioning itself as a 21st-century, technology-driven metropolis. But you'll still find a healthy dash of *grit*, *counter-culture* and *eclecticism*.

And when you're done gallivanting around the cocktail bars and farm-fresh restaurants, the cosy comedy spots and arthouse cinemas? You'll find plenty of salty-air *outdoor delights* to clear away the cobwebs. — (M)

Contents
—— Navigating
the city

Use the key below to
help navigate the guide
section by section.

(H) Hotels

(F) Food and
drink

(R) Retail

(T) Things
we'd buy

(E) Essays

(C) Culture

(D) Design and
architecture

(S) Sport and
fitness

(W) Walks

(O) Out of
town

Map
—— The city at a glance

San Franciscans often refer to their city as being 7×7 (miles) in a loving nod to its petite size. While it may not feel all that small when surveyed from the top of a hill, due to its peninsula location the city is in fact relatively compact.

Most of the action takes place on the city's northern and eastern fringes, with galleries, restaurants and businesses concentrated around the Financial District, North Beach and the Civic Center. South of Market (Soma) features an endless line of warehouses inhabited by technology big-hitters such as Twitter, Pinterest and Airbnb, while there are stellar retail offerings in both the Mission District and Hayes Valley. Plus outliers such as the Dogpatch, Outer Sunset, Inner Richmond and Outer Richmond are worthy of exploration for their tasty restaurants and up-and-coming shops and galleries.

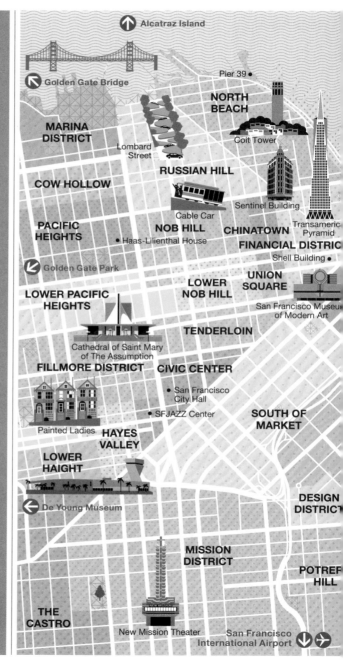

Alcatraz Island
Golden Gate Bridge
Pier 39
NORTH BEACH
MARINA DISTRICT
Coit Tower
Lombard Street
RUSSIAN HILL
COW HOLLOW
Cable Car
Sentinel Building
PACIFIC HEIGHTS
NOB HILL
CHINATOWN
Transamerica Pyramid
Haas-Lilienthal House
FINANCIAL DISTRICT
Golden Gate Park
Shell Building
UNION SQUARE
LOWER NOB HILL
LOWER PACIFIC HEIGHTS
San Francisco Museum of Modern Art
TENDERLOIN
Cathedral of Saint Mary of The Assumption
FILLMORE DISTRICT
CIVIC CENTER
San Francisco City Hall
SFJAZZ Center
SOUTH OF MARKET
Painted Ladies
HAYES VALLEY
LOWER HAIGHT
De Young Museum
DESIGN DISTRICT
MISSION DISTRICT
POTRERO HILL
THE CASTRO
New Mission Theater
San Francisco International Airport

0 | 500m N

MBARCADERO

Ferry Building
Marketplace

San Francisco – Oakland
Bay Bridge

● Pier 24 Photography

**SOUTH
BEACH**

AT&T Park

MISSION BAY

DOGPATCH

● Minnesota Street Project

● Sonoma   ● Napa

**SAN PABLO
BAY**

● San Rafael

● Muir Woods
National Monument   ● Berkeley

● Sausalito

● Oakland

SAN FRANCISCO

 San Francisco
International
Airport

Palo Alto ●

PACIFIC OCEAN

Cupertino ●

0 | 5km N

Need to know
—— Get to grips with the basics

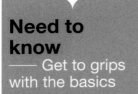

Want to know how to talk like a San Franciscan, navigate your way up and down the rolling streetscape, get to grips with the different neighbourhoods and prepare yourself for a meeting with a fellow called Karl? Read on for our fast facts and top tips for visitors to Fog City.

Neighbourhoods
The city's character

Explore the city on foot and you'll be rewarded with outstanding panoramas and the chance to feel the charming shifts in character as you glide from one neighbourhood to the next. Many San Franciscans worry that this vibrant diversity is being diluted but the hippie vibe of the Haight-Ashbury, the rainbow pride of The Castro and the sunbleached beach hair of the Outer Sunset are all still alive and thriving. And while neighbourhoods such as the Mission and Soma are rapidly filling with technology companies and their employees, other previously forgotten enclaves such as the Dogpatch, Tenderloin and Inner Richmond are experiencing spirited revivals.

Seismology
Ready to rumble

The city's proximity to the San Andreas Fault means that it's no stranger to seismic shifts. The most catastrophic of these was the 1906 Great San Francisco Earthquake, a 7.9 magnitude quake and subsequent fire that devastated the city. As a result, pre-1906 buildings are hard to find – and those that did survive later endured the 6.9 magnitude Loma Prieta quake of 1989, which killed 67 people and caused more than $5bn worth of damage. Beyond toppling the city and inspiring doomsday fanatics and Hollywood films, this seismic activity has informed the design of many landmarks, including the De Young Museum, Oakland Bay Bridge and city hall.

This could go horribly wrong...

Topography
Mind your step

The US method of planning a city to a grid system doesn't lend itself well to the relentless undulation of San Francisco's 70-plus hills; bear this in mind when judging distances from A to B. On paper, those neat grids make navigating seem easy but in reality the topography can be a little disorientating. The terrain function on your digital map will prove useful and, although the hills may at times break your spirit, the views really are spectacular.

Lingo
Acceptable appellations

If you want to blend in with the residents, resist the urge to refer to the city as San Fran. While this nickname is widely used elsewhere, it may be met with contempt when used in the company of native San Franciscans. (Before you ask, Frisco is also a no-go.) The safest bet is simply San Francisco or, if your propensity to find a pet name can't be quelled, try SF or The City; the latter is an indication of San Francisco's sway in the Bay Area.

Weather
June gloom

The fog is so common here that it has its own name – and Twitter account. Karl the Fog rolls in during summer when hot air over the land rises and cold air from the Pacific rushes in. These brilliantly theatrical scenes bring a drastic drop in temperature, so carry a few extra layers of clothing at all times. Then there are the microclimates: people parade in one neighbourhood wearing short shorts, while in another hoodies shroud hunched forms. Again, pack layers.

Green spaces
Out and about

San Francisco has more green spaces than you can poke with a hiking pole. Within easy reach of the city centre, labyrinthine tracks weave their way through the rugged Presidio, while craggy coastal paths and dark dunes run along the city's western edge. And that's not to mention the many manicured pockets small and large, from the Golden Gate Park to Washington Square. You may be visiting a city but you certainly won't find yourself short of grass.

You can see for miles! Wait, where's Monochan?

Silicon Valley
Chips with everything

Located around Stanford University in Palo Alto, Silicon Valley encompasses a large portion of the southern Bay Area. Cities such as Palo Alto, San José, Mountain View, Menlo Park and Cupertino host leading technology innovators, including Apple, Facebook and Google.

This concentration of industry is thought to date back to 1939, when a Stanford professor encouraged former students William Hewlett and David Packard to found their own electronics brand. A spate of manufacturers and innovators followed and the area was dubbed Silicon Valley after the material used for semiconductors in electronics. Some workers still commute from San Francisco (about a 40-minute drive) but more are moving to these smaller cities so their restaurant, cultural and retail offerings are on the up. The hotel scene could still do with a little more love though.

Tipping
Service charges

As in all big US cities, tipping is a given: expect 20 per cent on a restaurant bill. San Francisco takes its service industry seriously. A city mandate means that restaurants must provide employee healthcare (normally covered by a surcharge on your bill), ensuring good staff retention. When ordering at a bar it's standard to tip at least a dollar a drink, while a few dollars for taxi drivers (hailed services, not ride-share) and hotel staff is the norm.

Technology's impact
Rising tension

Disparity between those who work in technology and those who don't is increasing in the city. It's not uncommon for freshly graduated software engineers to earn $100,000 as their starting salary and such large disposable incomes have steepened the cost of living in San Francisco, with high rents forcing out longstanding residents and driving up restaurant and retail prices. While the technology sector is making the city competitive in business, it's simultaneously suppressing its prized diversity, liberalism and cultural girth. It will be interesting to see what city hall proposes for a cohesive relationship between the city and its big industry.

Bay Area
The bigger picture

Before we go any further, we should take a moment to explain why we've chosen to keep the scope of this guide within the city bounds of San Francisco. The San Francisco Bay Area encompasses the nine counties of Sonoma, Napa, Solano, Marin, San Francisco, San Mateo, Contra Costa, Alameda and Santa Clara, which include the cities of Berkeley, Oakland, San Jose and Palo Alto. Therefore, we decided to focus on the urban landscape of San Francisco itself but as a love letter to its picturesque neighbours, we've included a teaser of some tempting spots out of town (*see page 134*) should you find a day or two to explore the really rather seductive Bay Area.

Hotels
── Get a room

San Francisco punches well above its weight in many areas, which is why its relative dearth of decent hotels is so surprising. Partly this has been due to limited space and expensive real estate but thankfully there are signs that the hospitality scene is beginning to work around that. For starters, a host of hotels have been given much-needed facelifts and there are whispers that a few bigger-name and better-quality brands are coming to town.

San Francisco has long had one thing going for its hospitality scene: variety. From the sleek design of the Tilden to the intimate and exclusive club setting of The Battery, via the old-world palaces that hark back to the height of the city's golden age and a couple of lofty piles set within parkland, there's certainly no shortage of choice.

Ⓜ
Tilden, Tenderloin
Taste maker

The Tilden took a punt when it came to location: eschewing the city's "easy" neighbourhoods, it plumped for the gritty Tenderloin area. That shouldn't scare off prospective guests, however; put simply, this is one of the most tasteful places you could choose to stay in the city. Plus, a couple of blocks from Union Square, it's right in the thick of it.

Open since the start of 2017 – and designed by New York's Studio Tack – it has a mid-century feel, with plenty of wood in the lobby and a skylight (long covered during the building's previous incarnation as the Hotel Mark Twain). Be sure to drop by the in-house café, with brews by Equator Coffee and pastries by bakery Jane. As for the rooms, they're smartly decked out in black, white and grey with plenty of storage space, faucets by Waterworks and toiletries from Malin+Goetz. Plus, grab a drink or dinner at the adjoining bar and restaurant, The Douglas Room, from the folk behind Hotel G's Benjamin Cooper restaurant (*see page 42*).
*345 Taylor Street, 94102
+ 1 415 673 2332
tildenhotel.com*

MONOCLE COMMENT: The Tilden strives to engage the community, supporting nearby organisations and hosting local speakers at events. There's also art by San Franciscan Daniel Phill.

New and improved

The traditional oranges, reds and blacks of old Japantown establishment Hotel Kabuki have been given a total refresh. Cupboards have lost their doors, tones have turned earthy and there's now a distinctly contemporary pop-art feel.
jdvhotels.com

②
Palace Hotel, Soma
Ahead of the crowd

The Palace was the first luxury
hotel in the city when it opened in
1875. It was cutting-edge for the
time, a bricks-and-mortar building
when others were made of timber
and with telegraph communication
on every floor.

Fast-forward to today and the
rooms have a contemporary twist
– all have smart headboards with
leather tufting and some feature
Toto washlets – without letting
you forget that you're staying
in a traditional hotel. The suites
have high ceilings and plenty
of light and the communal spaces
are well-designed: the Garden
Court restaurant resides in a
grand, open-plan hallway and
is overlooked by a roof made of
some 70,000 panels of glass, while
the beautiful Pied Piper Bar is
dominated by Maxfield Parrish's
painting of the same name.
2 New Montgomery Street, 94105
+1 415 512 1111
sfpalace.com

MONOCLE COMMENT: The hotel
retains a certain old-school charm
(solid-brass doorknobs for all
rooms, for instance) and also has
an indoor pool – a rarity in the city.

③
Inn at the Presidio, Presidio
All about that base

Located in the city's vast national park, this hotel is particularly popular with outdoorsy types and the romantic-break crowd. But even if you're on business it serves as a peaceful retreat.

Housed in a building that dates back to 1903 – the former barracks of bachelor officers when the Presidio was an army base (*see page 106*) – the hotel feels a bit like a country lodge. The determination of curator Julie Coyle to delve into the Presidio's past is notable. Rooms have shadowboxes of memorabilia, from old postcards to rusted keys, and many feature utilitarian framed beds (it's all about the mattress); elsewhere, framed black-and-white photos with embossed metal ID tags for captions show army types in skimpy shorts. For more privacy there's the Funston House, a four-bedroom Victorian annexe.
42 Moraga Avenue (on Main Post), 94129
+1 415 800 7356
innatthepresidio.com

MONOCLE COMMENT: The Presidio Social Club – also known as Building 563 – does an excellent *bucatini fra diavolo* (pasta with a spicy tomato sauce).

Lounge around
——
Sit back and relax in the lobby with a cocktail

④
The St Regis San Francisco, Soma
Chain reaction

You can't go wrong with The St Regis, which offers the same service that you would find in any of the brand's other metropolis hotels, from a morning fix of French-press coffee to a round-the-clock butler service, should you require it.

Designed by Yabu Pushelberg in a colour palette of white and cream, the hotel feels modern but is undoubtedly slanted towards business travellers. Each room is a decent size and there are some beautiful suites to choose from, such as the Metropolitan Suite with its alluring hint of navy. During your stay don't miss the Art of Tea, a daily spread of nibbles hosted between 14.00 and 16.00 (champagne is optional). The contemporary Grill restaurant is also worth a gander.
125 3rd Street, 94103
+1 415 284 4000
stregissanfrancisco.com

MONOCLE COMMENT: The St Regis is perfect for those who enjoy being pampered: there's 24-hour room service, a daily newspaper delivery and – if you so fancy – an LCD television screen in the bathroom.

⑤
Hotel G, Union Square
Youth of today

It may be located in a traditionally touristy area just off Union Square but there isn't much else that's traditional about Hotel G. Since opening in 2014, this Thai-owned stop-in has injected some youth and fun into the hospitality scene.

The interiors are industrial mid-century but with enough personality to keep them from feeling stark. The lobby is filled with art and plants, while the 153 rooms (one of which is a suite) have oversized headboards and tasteful details such as light fixtures from Portland's Schoolhouse Electric and radios from Tivoli. Keep an eye out for the tongue-in-cheek signs dotted around the hotel – "Things can get hot and heavy" in the gym – and be sure to sip a snifter at the Benjamin Cooper hotel bar (*see page 42*).
386 Geary Street, 94102
+1 877 828 4478
hotelgsanfrancisco.com

MONOCLE COMMENT: Hotel G is worth considering for a small business gathering. The conference room isn't big but it's naturally lit and nicely decked out with foliage.

Sitting pretty
—
Pull up a pew on the wrap-around porch

6

Cavallo Point Lodge, Sausalito
Get out of town

We're stretching the boundaries of San Francisco a little with this one but it would be remiss to leave it out. Located just outside the city on the northern side of the Golden Gate Bridge (many of the rooms look directly onto it), this hotel is a sensitively restored turn-of-the-century military building not too dissimilar in its concept to The Inn at the Presidio (*see page 18*).

Choose between the original house, with its authentic tin ceiling and fireplaces, and the hillside new-build rooms with their floor-to-ceiling windows, spectacular views and radiant-heat floors for those slightly chilly nights. There's also the Murray Circle restaurant, optional cooking classes, yoga sessions and hiking in the nearby national park. In short, it would be easy to stay on this side of the bridge for your entire trip.
601 Murray Circle, 94965
+1 888 651 2003
cavallopoint.com

MONOCLE COMMENT: There is 2,700 sq m of indoor and outdoor event space here. With those views, it's not a bad place for a meeting – or somewhere to come and forget about the office altogether, come to think of it.

⑦
The Battery, Financial District
Join the club

The Battery may be a private members club but you can get around that caveat by staying in one of its 14 rooms or the penthouse suite, which are open to the public. The bedrooms are spacious and slightly masculine – think brown-leather armchairs, large TVs and often plenty of exposed brickwork – and the bathrooms are kitted out with stone tiles and toiletries by Molton Brown.

A stay here comes complete with full membership privileges, including access to the beautiful library, which feels like a cross between a hunting lodge and a boat (ships' lights hang between the spines and stuffed birds perch on the chandelier). There are several bars, as well as the Living Room restaurant and a garden with views of the Transamerica Pyramid. Plus there's a tranquil spa and well-equipped gym.
717 Battery Street, 94111
+1 415 230 8000
thebatterysf.com

MONOCLE COMMENT: Look out for the vibrant Tracey Snelling artwork near the library.

⑧
Kimpton Buchanan, Japantown
Past and present

This bankable option is located between Pacific Heights and Japantown – not far from Fillmore Street, which is good for both shopping and eating.

The hotel draws on the local area for its design inspiration. In the refurbished lobby, some 3,000 Japanese whiskey bottles hang from the ceiling near a curved brown-leather sofa. The 131 rooms are modern but with a hint of Japanese heritage, particularly through their use of *shibori* (think tie-dye but without the hippie baggage) on the accent pillows, the fantastic navy-and-white room robes and the carpet and wallpaper in the hallway. Another nice touch? The patio with fire pit, open until 22.00.
1800 Sutter Street, 94115
+1 415 921 4000
thebuchananhotel.com

MONOCLE COMMENT: The Kimpton Buchanan may have changed but the old-school hotel restaurant has been around for more than 40 years and is known for its *shabu-shabu* hotpot dish.

⑩

Proper Hotel, Civic Center
Lovingly restored flatiron

Located along San Francisco's Market Street, Proper Hotel is the latest tenant to inhabit a historic beaux arts "flatiron" building dating back to 1904. For this flagship of the fledgling California-based Proper Hospitality, no detail has been overlooked: the crumbling exterior and lobby have been painstakingly restored, down to the plaster mouldings and Carrara marble floors.

The 131 rooms have been furnished by interior designer Kelly Wearstler and all feature Aesop bathroom products and Aireloom mattresses (handmade in California). Be sure to try at least one of the four dining options, which include a lobby commissary and rooftop lounge. These alone are good enough to warrant a stay.
45 McAllister Street, 94102
+1 415 735 7777
properhotel.com

MONOCLE COMMENT: There are some lovely views on offer at the Proper Hotel: take a junior suite and you can gaze out at Market Street on one side and the Twin Peaks on the other.

⑨

Fairmont San Francisco, Nob Hill
Grand standing

Few places show the wealth and grandeur of San Francisco's gilded age better than this huge beaux arts pile atop Nob Hill. It was designed as a residence by US architect Stanford White but various factors, including the 1906 earthquake, meant that it was never used for its intended purpose.

A hotel since 1907 (according to a later design by Julia Morgan), the Fairmont is steeped in history and in 1945 the UN Charter was drafted in one of its rooms. It has a wonderfully kitsch tiki bar, the Tonga Room, complete with a boat floating in its own pool, and has been here for more than 70 years – long enough for the decor to fall in and out of fashion (and come back in again). The rooms are more modern than you might expect, due to a recent refresh. For sweeping vistas of the bay, request a spot in the newer – though slightly less attractive – tower.
950 Mason Street, 94108
+1 415 772 5000
fairmont.com

Fine hotel dining
———
Hankering after a two-Michelin-starred dining experience? Better hit up the Taj Campton Place's restaurant, where you can get the full white-tablecloth, "Cal-Indian" experience from chef Srijith Gopinathan.
tajcamptonplace.com

MONOCLE COMMENT: Illustrious guests such as John F Kennedy, Bill Clinton and Mick Jagger have all stayed in the Penthouse Suite.

Food and drink
—— Edible options

Locally sourced, market-driven, farm-to-table: these core tenets of San Francisco's food scene may seem tired but, with farmland and wine country so close by, they're upheld with earnestness. Chefs regularly visit multiple markets a week and restaurants serving out-of-season produce are shunned.

But while there's an array of fine-dining destinations, this isn't a fine-dining city. Three-star restaurants spawn casual spinoffs that often become more popular than the originals: the young technology community has little interest in the fussy or stuffy. There's also a wealth of street food – especially in the Mission, where the burritos are unrivalled elsewhere in the US. We hope you're hungry.

①
Tadich Grill, Financial District
A piece of history

Founded in 1849 as a coffee stand in the Financial District (when the Financial District was still a series of wharves), Tadich Grill is San Francisco's oldest restaurant. "At least half of this menu goes back 100 years," says current owner Mike Buich – that's around the time that his grandfather took over the restaurant.

Signature dishes include Australian lobster tail and *cioppino*, a seafood stew traditionally made by fishermen. Head chef Wil Going sources his fish from local suppliers.
240 California Street, 94111
+1 415 391 1849
tadichgrill.com

2

Outerlands, Outer Sunset
Beach culture, embodied

Outerlands is the epicentre of
Outer Sunset's new wave of cool
beach culture. The brunch menu
is luscious and attracts a large
weekend crowd (reservations are
encouraged) but dinner is when
you'll get a better sense of the
locals: surfers, artists and families.
  The menu changes regularly
but the bread is a constant. Owner
Dave Muller learned from the
baker at Tartine (*see pages 30 and
31*), making adjustments for Outer
Sunset's more humid climate,
resulting in a moist, chewy boule
with a crunchy exterior.
*4001 Judah Street, 94122
+1 415 661 6140
outerlandssf.com*

Don't worry,
I promise
I'll give you
half...

③
Rintaro Izakaya, Mission District
Dreams of Japan

Stepping through Rintaro's wooden gate, which chef and owner Sylvan Mishima Brackett (*pictured*) made himself, is like stepping out of the US and into Japan. Brackett designed the space in partnership with Frost Tsuji Architects, reflecting the traditional approach to craftsmanship that he inherited from his father, who studied as a Japanese temple architect before emigrating. The restaurant interior features clay walls that were packed by hand and a bar top made from a single slab of cedar.

Brackett's cooking is informed by the years he spent as Alice Waters' assistant at Chez Panisse. Nosh on sashimi and yakitori while you wait for the main act: a big bowl of hand-rolled udon with locally sourced accoutrements.
82 14th Street, 94103
+1 415 589 7022
izakayarintaro.com

Must-try
Oysters from Hog Island, Embarcadero
These bivalves, plucked from Tomales Bay, have a delicate saline flavour that's easy on the palate. They're available at many restaurants in the city or you can enjoy them freshly shucked at Hog Island's all-day café in the Ferry Building.
ferrybuildingmarketplace.com

⑤
In Situ, Soma
Originality redefined

In Situ debuted to great acclaim as part of the reopening of SFMoma (*see page 93*). Chef Corey Lee uses the concept of a museum devoted to the dishes that have shaped modern cuisine: think wood sorrel and sheep's milk yogurt from Noma in 2005 or *kalbi jjim* (braised short ribs) from LA Son in 2013.

Dishes are replicated impeccably. This may sound like forgery but the question is about context: what happens when you separate the sensory experience of eating a dish from the setting and time it was originally served?
151 3rd Street, 94103
+1 415 941 6050
insitu.sfmoma.org

④
The Big 4, Nob Hill
Decadent history

In both name and spirit, The Big 4 pays homage to the railroad tycoons whose influence dominated San Francisco in the late 19th century. The dining room is masculine and lavish, with emerald-green leather banquettes and white tablecloths, and features a grand piano.

The space underwent renovations in 2014 and the menu was lightened up when Kevin Scott took over the kitchen and brought a modern touch to the classic US dishes. Perfect for a martini and a steak, with live music, a roaring fire and plenty of people-watching.
1075 California Street, 94108
+1 415 771 1140
big4restaurant.com

Critically acclaimed

01 Coi, Financial District:
Founded by Daniel
Patterson, Coi debuted
on the World's Best list
at 49 in 2014. It's now
run by Matthew Kirkley
and has shifted its focus
to seafood.
coirestaurant.com

02 Saison, South Beach:
This restaurant has
enjoyed two years in the
top 50 under founding
chef Joshua Skenes, as
of 2017. With the tasting
menu costing nearly $400,
it's the city's priciest table.
saisonsf.com

03 Benu, South Beach: Run
by former chef de cuisine
at The French Laundry,
Corey Lee, Benu serves 11
globally inspired courses.
benusf.com

*Eek! The food here
really is fresh*

6
Foreign Cinema, Mission District
Dinner and a show

Zuni Café alumni Gayle Pirie
and John Clark took over Foreign
Cinema in 2001, when the dotcom economy was going bust
and chefs still clung to using off-
season produce. But their vision
for a multifaceted, sensual dining
experience in an old cinema gave
rise to one of the most consistently
lauded restaurants in the city.
   Honouring the original use
of the venue, a nightly film is
screened via a projector on the
patio; there's plenty on the menu
to make for moreish film snacks.
2534 Mission Street, 94110
+1 415 648 7600
foreigncinema.com

⑦
Hook Fish Co, Outer Sunset
Stellar seafood

Inspired by casual seafood markets
in their hometown of Newport
Beach, Orange County, surfers
Beau Caillouette (*pictured, left*)
and Christian Morabito (*pictured,
middle*) teamed up to create a
sustainable seafood business. After
building a following via catered
events and pop-ups, they opened
this permanent location in 2017.
    The restaurant-cum-fish market
has a whiteboard citing the origin
of each fish, down to the vessel that
caught it. Head chef Luke Johnson
(*pictured, right*) dishes up ceviche,
fish tacos, crab cakes and an
especially memorable poke burrito.
4542 Irving Street, 94122
hookfishco.com

⑧
Petit Crenn, Hayes Valley
French fancy

After earning two Michelin
stars for her Atelier Crenn, chef
Dominique Crenn opened this
more casual concept restaurant in
2015. Inspired by her upbringing
in France, it's part bistro, part
dinner party – and all French.
    The menu is seafood and
vegetables only, served in dishes
to be shared among the table. The
principal fish is presented before
it's cooked and, in true French
style, it's followed by salad and
cheese. The seven-course tasting
menu is by reservation but walk-ins
may order à la carte.
609 Hayes Street, 94102
+1 415 864 1744
petitcrenn.com

⑨
State Bird Provisions,
Fillmore District
Going solo

Husband and wife Stuart Brioza
and Nicole Krasinski made waves
with State Bird Provisions, earning
a Michelin star and a James Beard
award almost at once.
    Dinner is served in two ways:
"provisions", which are small bites
offered on carts, dim sum style,
and "commandables", larger dishes
available à la carte. Included in the
latter grouping is the namesake dish:
deep-fried quail, the Californian
state bird. The service style and tiny
dishes make this an ideal option for
adventurous solo diners.
1529 Fillmore Street, 94115
+1 415 795 1272
statebirdsf.com

10

Boulettes Larder and Boulibar,
Embarcadero
Must-try mezze

Boulettes Larder encompasses two
dining rooms and a shop. Take in
Bay Bridge views during the day in
the Kallosturin-designed original
space or cosy up in the evening at
Boulibar, where pizzas and pitta
breads are fired in the wood oven.

For lunch and dinner, both
offer a classic mezze, with more
adventurous options such as cumin-
marinated beetroots and melon with
chilli and sea salt. The sophisticated
ambience makes both venues ideal
for business associates or clients.
Suites 48 and 35, 1 Ferry Building,
94111
+1 415 399 1155
bouletteslarder.com

11

Out the Door, Lower
Pacific Heights
Veritable Vietnamese

This casual spinoff of the iconic
The Slanted Door offers the best
of its sister restaurant's menu
without the fuss. Charles Phan, the
chef and restaurateur behind both,
came to the US as a child refugee
from Vietnam in the 1970s. He
opened his original restaurant as a
family business and the familial feel
permeates the Bush Street space.

Vietnamese flavours and local
ingredients are front and centre in
every dish. Don't miss the crispy
imperial rolls, which complement
everything else on the menu.
2232 Bush Street, 94115
+1 415 923 9575
outthedoors.com

12

Cala, Civic Center
Minimalist Mexican

Chef Gabriela Cámara left Mexico
City to open this elegant but
unfussy affair and some of San
Francisco's leading food critics now
claim that it's the best Mexican
restaurant in the country.

Start with a mezcal cocktail
and seafood tostadas. The mains
are best shared: the rockfish *a la
talla* (served whole) is for two,
while the sweet potato with bone
marrow salsa negra is perfect for
passing around. For lunch, head
behind the restaurant to Tacos
Cala, which serves tacos *de guisado*
(with stewed fillings).
149 Fell Street, 94102
+1 415 660 7701
calarestaurant.com

Mexican meals

01 **La Taqueria, Mission District:** The burrito here dispenses with filler (rice) and includes only meat, pinto beans, avocado and salsa. It won the James Beard America's Classics award in 2017.
taqueriasanfrancisco.com

02 **La Palma Mexicatessen, Mission District:** Open since the 1950s, this market draws people for its handmade tortillas, which you can take home or enjoy hot off the griddle.
lapalmasf.com

03 **Gallardo's, Mission District:** There's more to Mexican food than tacos. Gallardo's speciality is *pozole*, which bursts with corn flavour and meaty broth.
+1 415 436 9387

04 **Tommy's, Outer Richmond:** This joint has served the best margaritas in town since the 1960s. Come for 100 per cent agave tequila, stay for the classic Mexican fare.
+1 415 387 4347

05 **Celia's by the Beach, Outer Sunset:** A favourite among the Outer Sunset locals, this café was the first in a small chain of family-owned restaurants.
celiasbythebeach.com

⑬
Tartine Manufactory,
Mission District
Made on the premises

The duo behind Tartine Bakery opened the Manufactory as more than a restaurant: the bread served at both establishments is made in the onsite dough room and proofing chamber.

The rest of the Manufactory's menu is brought to life in a minimalist kitchen. Breakfast, lunch and dinner include bread-focused options such as a brioche jam bun, a porchetta sandwich and smørrebrød, while the wine list celebrates natural methods.
595 Alabama Street, 94110
+1 415 757 0007
tartinemanufactory.com

Baked good

Tartine Bakery, the city's most celebrated pastry provider, continues to crank out French classics in its original café on Guerrero Street. Stop by for a pillowy, crunchy butter croissant or a peppery *gougère* (cheese puff).
tartinebakery.com

Must-try
Roast chicken from Zuni Café, Civic Center
More than a dish, this is an atmospheric experience. It takes 60 minutes to prepare (snack on oysters while you wait) and when it comes, the skin is crisped to perfection. Served with a bread salad.
zunicafe.com

⑭
Frances, The Castro
Neighbourhood sensation

Chef Melissa Perello opened Frances in 2009 to immediate acclaim and reservations are just as hard to come by today. Walk-ins are seated at the counter, which features the typical Californian view of a palm tree.

The narrow dining room obliges you to get cosy with your neighbours, which is part of the charm. As you settle in for a comforting, memorable meal, start with the *panisse frites* (chickpea fries) and sip on the house wine, blended for Frances and sold by the ounce.
3870 17th Street, 94114
+1 415 621 3870
frances-sf.com

⑮
Cotogna, Jackson Square
Hot-ticket trattoria

When Michael and Lindsay Tusk moved their three Michelin-starred restaurant Quince to Jackson Square in 2009, they took on its adjoining café space, which became Cotogna, an inspired take on Italy's rustic trattoria.

Simplicity is the guiding principle here, with pasta and pizza the stars of the menu, while the wine list is split into three price points and styled on a single page. With its corner exposure to tree-lined streets and a warm, brick interior, Cotogna's romantic dining room is an ideal date spot.
460 Pacific Avenue, 94133
+1 415 775 8508
cotognasf.com

Farm-to-table institutions

Seasonal, fresh-from-the-farm food is nothing new in San Francisco; in fact, it's been a guiding principle of the local culture since the 1970s.

01 Greens Restaurant, Marina District: Opened in 1979, Greens was originally part of the San Francisco Zen Center, sharing land with Green Gulch farms. Chef Annie Somerville continues to source produce from Green Gulch for use in her all-vegetarian menu.
greensrestaurant.com

02 Zuni Café, Civic Center: What started as a tiny rustic café serving fresh guacamole and Caesar salad is one of the city's most beloved institutions. In 1987, chef Judy Rodgers took over and had a wood-fired oven built.
zunicafe.com

03 Nopa, Western Addition: This place has been setting food trends since it opened in 2006. Its signature dishes are constants on the menu but chef Laurence Jossel also keeps it fresh. He visits as many as five farmers' markets a week for the best produce.
nopasf.com

⑯
Tosca Café, Financial District
A modern classic

Once a watering hole for libertines and Beats, Tosca was reopened in 2014 by April Bloomfield and Ken Friedman, the restaurateurs behind The Spotted Pig in New York.

Both the dishes and decor pay homage to the neighbourhood's Italian-US roots. The dining room is cosy, with red banquettes, while the bar is lively, populated by foodies, businesspeople and restaurant industry folks – perhaps because it's one of the only spots in the city that serves dinner until 01.00. The focaccia is essential, even just as a side order.
242 Columbus Avenue, 94133
+1 415 986 9651
toscacafesf.com

⑰
Lers Ros, Civic Center
Local favourite

In a city known for its Asian food, chef Tom Narupon Silargorn's Lers Ros is the standard-bearer for Thai restaurants. Beloved by locals for authentic flavours and exotic meat dishes such as *pla duk pad phed* (catfish) and *pad kra prow moo krob* (pork belly), it also has a critically acclaimed wine list.

Silargorn has established a small empire in San Francisco. His newer locations in Hayes Valley and the Mission offer sleek interiors but the lively bar and cosier seating in the original Civic Center spot best reflect the chef's soulfulness.
730 Larkin Street, 94109
+1 415 931 6917
lersros.com

Late-night special

Tosca caters to late-night diners with an off-menu gem, available only after 22.30: spaghetti and meatballs. Don't bother asking for it earlier than that because the servers are very strict about the temporal rule.
toscacafesf.com

18
Rich Table, Hayes Valley
Californian synergy

Opened in 2012, Rich Table still
packs in a nightly crowd and serves
dishes emblematic of Northern
California's food culture.
　The flavours and methods
reflect myriad influences (Japanese,
European, Californian, fine
dining and street food) with shiso
layered onto Mediterranean-style
dishes and tempura replacing
conventional US frying. The
signature bite is the porcini
"doughnut", like a bao bun but
more pillowy and less sticky; served
with warm, gooey raclette cheese
to complement its umami taste.
199 Gough Street, 94102
+1 415 355 9085
richtablesf.com

Lunch
Midday munchables

1
20th Century Café, Civic Center
Retro chic

Inspired by visits to Vienna,
Budapest and Prague, pastry
chef Michelle Polzine *(pictured)*
created this shop in the image of
central Europe's grand cafés. Her
expertly crafted baked goods are
accordingly the stars of the menu.
　The sunny interior has tables
custom-made to the European size,
which is much smaller than the
typical US version. You can spot
Polzine in the open kitchen, often
bopping along to the soundtrack
of a bygone era. It's a place to dine
in, so take a moment to enjoy the
kitsch and an espresso.
198 Gough Street, 94102
+1 415 621 2380
20thcenturycafe.com

Must-try
Crazy Crab'z sandwich from
AT&T Park, South Beach
This ballpark fare uses fresh
Dungeness crab and tomatoes
packed between two slices
of toasted and buttered
sourdough. If you're still hungry,
nab some garlic fries. Good
fodder for a sports stadium.
*sanfrancisco.giants.mlb.com/
sf/ballpark*

2

Wise Sons, Mission District
& Fillmore District
Heavenly bagels

Wise Sons' original lunch joint
opened in 2010 on 24th Street but
the Jewish deli reached its current
acclaim after setting up a bagelry in
2016. For a sit-down midday meal
head to the original location or, for
arguably the best bagel in town, try
the Fillmore Street bakery.

For the full California bagel
experience, order yours "dragged
through the garden" – that's to
say with layers of greens, radishes,
cucumber and pickled onion.
*3150 24th Street, 94110
+1 415 787 3354;
1520 Fillmore Street, 94115
+1 415 872 9046
wisesonsdeli.com*

Quick bites

Ask anyone to recommend a
budget-friendly dish in San
Francisco and you'll likely be
directed to a burrito joint. *Banh
mi* (Vietnamese sandwiches),
however, are just as delightful
and becoming increasingly
popular across the city.

01 Saigon Sandwich,
Tenderloin: San
Franciscans in the know
flock to this Tenderloin
dive for layer upon layer
of chicken, pork and pâté
on crunchy baguette.
+1 415 474 5698
02 Mr Banh Mi, Outer
Richmond: The family
behind Kim Son
Restaurant in Outer
Richmond opened this
sandwich shop right
across the street.
+1 415 463 6588
03 Dinosaurs, The Castro:
Slightly more highbrow
than the other spots on
our list, Dinosaurs offers
fixings such as jicama
and taro root on its
vegetarian sandwich.
dinosaursrestaurant.com

And then sum

With a large and longstanding
Chinese immigrant community,
San Francisco is home to a
wealth of authentic dim sum
restaurants. Head to Chinatown
or the Richmond for weekend
brunch among the locals but
be prepared to wait; the top
spots attract large crowds.

③
Bon, Nene, Mission District
French/Japanese oasis

Nestled on a residential block, Bon, Nene is an unassuming gem. The concept is Japanese, executed with French techniques: co-owners Stephanie Chan and Miu Furuta have created a space like your Parisian-by-way-of-Kyoto friend's apartment. It's perfect for an intimate lunch with an old friend or a solo escape from nearby destination restaurants.

The house speciality is a spin on gyoza, served in a delicate bunch bundled together by the crispy lace from the pan and available as part of the well-priced lunch plate.
2850 21st Street, 94110
+1 415 872 9332
bonnene.com

④
Darwin Café, Soma
Surprising sandwiches

Despite its shoebox size and tucked-away location, it's easy to spot Darwin Café – just look for the line. If it seems dauntingly long, don't fret; the international music and friendly staff will help the time pass quickly.

The menu is focused on hearty salads and innovative sandwiches: a turkey-and-prosciutto sandwich, for example, loaded with sweet onions, rocket and balsamic. If you're after something a little simpler, the kitchen offers a steady selection of classics on baguette including ham, gruyère and dijon.
212 Ritch Street, 94107
+1 415 800 8668
darwincafesf.com

⑤
Swan Oyster Depot, Nob Hill
Local legend

If there's one place in San Francisco that will always have a queue, it's Swan Oyster Depot. After more than 100 years of business, crowds still flock to this seafood destination and will wait for hours for one of 18 seats at the counter. Anthony Bourdain is a regular customer and it's an enduring favourite among even the city's most discerning food editors.

The attraction is two-fold: impeccably fresh seafood prepared in an unpretentious fashion, and the genuine hospitality of the Sancimino family, who've run Swan since 1946.
1517 Polk Street, 94109
+1 415 673 1101

Coffee shops
Caffeine injectors

② Mazarine Coffee, Financial District
Rare varieties

Mazarine Coffee was founded in 2014 when technology professional Hamid Rafati decided to follow his passion for coffee and switch careers. The name of the café references France's oldest public library.

Several coffee varieties from roasters in and around the Bay Area are available daily. The venue is work-friendly, with free wi-fi and power outlets, so tables can be hard to come by. Instead, nab a stool with a view of one of Market Street's busiest intersections.
720 Market Street, 94102
+1 415 398 7700
mazarinecoffee.com

① Sightglass, Mission District
Charming filter

While freelancers congregate at Sightglass's Soma flagship, laptops in tow, intimate conversations prevail in this second outpost, nestled on one of the Mission's most charming blocks.

It has a decidedly neighbourly feel and the coffee is roasted on-site, using a German Probat that's a petite version of the one in the original location. The chic clientele make for great people-watching, so cosy up on the tufted leather banquette with one of the signature filter coffees for a picturesque slice of the Mission life.
3014 20th Street, 94110
+1 415 641 1043
sightglasscoffee.com

Feeling blue?
———
With its HQ across the bay, eight cafés in the city and investment from the technology industry, Blue Bottle is San Francisco's flagship coffee brand. It's buying up small roasters to fuel expansion but don't miss the original cafés.
bluebottlecoffee.com

③
The Mill, Fillmore District
Baristas and baked goods

The Mill has had a line out the door since it opened in 2013. A collaboration between Four Barrel Coffee and Josey Baker Bread, the space is made for mingling. There's no wi-fi or customer-facing power outlets – rare for this technology-driven city.

The Mill is one of the city's original purveyors of fancy toast, with toppings such as almond butter and (of course) avocado mash. It also always offers a vegetarian sandwich at lunch and a pizza for dinner, the flavours of which change weekly.
736 Divisadero Street, 94117
+1 415 345 1953
themillsf.com

④
Saint Frank, Russian Hill
Community cup

Ritual Coffee Roasters alum Kevin Bohlin opened this bright-white café in 2013 to foster deeper connections between customers and their coffee. In an effort to buck the soulless commodification of coffee, the brand sources beans via direct relationships with producers around the world.

In the café, drinks are prepared using a custom-designed coffee machine that's built into the counter, allowing baristas to interact with customers rather than being hidden behind an espresso machine.
2340 Polk Street, 94109
+1 415 775 1619
saintfrankcoffee.com

Best buns

The city is known for its classic sourdough loaves but recently the artisanal baking scene has been on the rise.

01 **B Patisserie, Lower Pacific Heights:** Belinda Leong and Michel Suas offer pastries and tartines that marry the duo's French and Californian sensibilities.
bpatisserie.com

02 **Mr Holmes Bakehouse, Tenderloin:** This tiny spot created a frenzy for popularising the "cruffin", a croissant-muffin hybrid.
mrholmesbakehouse.com

03 **Le Marais, citywide:** A bakery-cum-bistro offering *pâtisserie* and *viennoiserie*. The butter croissants are a pastry purist's dream.
lemaraisbakery.com

04 **Neighbor Bakehouse, Dogpatch:** The smoked-fish-and-cream-cheese croissant here pays homage to the bagel and the special brioche tarts use seasonal produce.
neighborsf.com

05 **Marla, Outer Richmond:** Classic bagels (salt, sesame, poppy and "really seedy") with modern toppings (smoked trout and pickled vegetables).
marlabakery.com

Ice cream

San Franciscans love ice cream. Try Humphry Slocombe's Secret Breakfast (condensed milk, bourbon and cornflakes); Bi-Rite's elegant black sesame; or Gott's *fior di latte*.
humphryslocombe.com; biritecreamery.com; gotts.com

Food shops and markets
Pick up some produce

① China Live, Russian Hill
Upscale emporium

This Chinese emporium is home to a shop, restaurant and cocktail bar. The restaurant seats 120 but attentive service and a well-designed interior make for an intimate feel.

Food is prepared at four stations and bar seats at each afford views of the chefs. The tea shop brews teas direct from farmers in China and Taiwan, while retail shelves are filled with design-forward rice cookers and tea sets, non-GMO Chinese condiments and elegant cutlery.
644 Broadway, 94133
+1 415 788 8188
chinalivesf.com

② Ferry Building Marketplace, Embarcadero
Landmark market

Once a heavily trafficked transit hub for those commuting by ferry, this landmark fell into obscurity and disrepair for the second half of the 20th century. Following an extensive restoration, it reopened in 2003 as a hall for restaurants, food stands and events.

The Saturday farmers' market is the city's largest and includes pop-up stalls from nearby restaurants. Be sure to try the rotisserie chicken from the RoliRoti truck and the lox tartine from Cap'n Mike's Holy Smoke.
1 Ferry Building, 94111
+1 415 983 8030
ferrybuildingmarketplace.com

③

Bi-Rite Market, Mission District
Market force

Sam Mogannam grew up dusting shelves and mopping floors in his father's shop. He then became a chef before returning to take over the market in 1997 with his brother Raph and making it a hub for the food community.

"We brought a chef's mentality to the market," he says. "We buy for specific recipes that people are likely to make." The brand expanded into a Divisadero Street location in 2013 and both draw customers seeking fresh produce from regional farms, speciality products and Bi-Rite Creamery's ice cream.
3639 18th Street, 94110
+1 415 241 9760
biritemarket.com

④

William Cross Wine Merchants, Russian Hill
Worldly wines

Every bottle you see on the shelves of this Russian Hill wine shop is hand-selected by the staff, who taste nearly 10,000 bottles a year to stock the place. And they don't just have expensive taste; the owner takes pride in putting as much thought into the selection of $15 bottles as he does into that of $50 ones.

Nestled in the back of the shop is a tasting bar, where a daily flight and wines by the glass are served. Stop by on a Wednesday night to mingle with locals and winemakers at one of the casual tasting events.
2253 Polk Street, 94109
+1 415 346 1314
wmcross.com

⑤

Little Vine, North Beach
Picnic provisions

The floor-to-ceiling shelves in this pint-sized speciality deli are packed full of cheese, wine, charcuterie, jams, crackers and other gourmet treats. The on-staff cheesemonger will happily assist you in choosing from the international selection of cheeses and let you try before you buy. Wine tastings are held every Thursday evening.

Make this a pit-stop on your way to nearby Washington Square Park for a picnic or pick up a snack for the hike up to Coit Tower (*see page 108*).
1541 Grant Avenue, 94133
+1 415 738 2221
shoplittlevine.com

Alfresco eats

As property prices have skyrocketed, trucks have become an increasingly notable part of San Francisco's food scene. Off the Grid's seasonal series of outdoor dining events brings together food stands, music and entertainment in picnic settings around the city.
offthegrid.com

Drinks
Top tipples

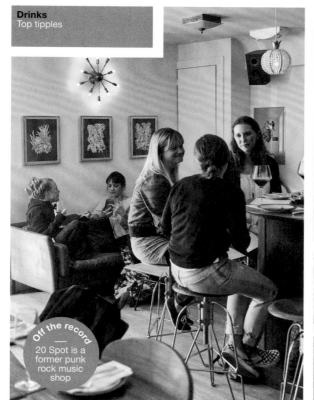

Off the record
—
20 Spot is a former punk rock music shop

(1)
20 Spot, Mission District
Wine club

After running Bacchus, a tiny wine bar atop Russian Hill, for more than a decade, Bodhi Freedom (*pictured, above*) leapt at the opportunity for a new venture based in his longtime Mission neighbourhood. Enlisting architect Wylie Price, he soon transformed a vacant shop from a dingy space into a chic wine bar.

"The idea was to make a clubhouse," he says. The wine list is mostly European, catering to the area's inquisitive clientele. "People come here to get turned onto things that they aren't familiar with."
3565 20th Street, 94110
+1 415 624 3140
20spot.com

041

② Benjamin Cooper, Nob Hill
Speakeasy style

Hidden behind an unmarked door at the Hotel G (*see page 20*), Benjamin Cooper offers safe haven from the masses in Union Square. The tone is decadent, with a velvet-and-gold interior, lush ingredients in the cocktails, and a snack menu that consists solely of raw oysters.

The drinks are both seasonal (look for beetroot juice in the spring and torched apple slices in autumn) and strong, often including several different spirits and liqueurs. Perch at the bar to see the bartenders constantly shaking cocktails or shucking oysters.

398 Geary Street, 94102
+1 415 654 5061
benjamincoopersf.com

③ High Treason, Inner Richmond
Lo-fi wine bar

Sommeliers Michael Ireland and John Vuong created High Treason as an antidote to the formality of the Michelin-starred restaurant scene. The selection of wine, beer and small bites is elevated and interesting, while the setting is inclusive and unpretentious.

This is one of the only spots in town that has as many interesting European wines – think funky, barnyard jura – as Californian ones. Pleasingly, there's also a regular crowd that's more diverse than the predominantly young and single technology demographic elsewhere.

443 Clement Street, 94118
+1 415 742 5256
hightreasonsf.com

④ Trick Dog, Mission District
Creative concoctions

Trick Dog has been winning awards for its quirky and complex cocktails since it opened in 2013. The hospitality group behind it, known as The Bon Vivants, dreams up new themes, content and designs for the menu twice a year.

"The ideas are pretty wide ranging," says partner Morgan Schick. Past menus have included a calendar of dogs, an astrology map and an art book showcasing San Francisco murals. The bar also offers copies of the menu for sale and donates a portion of the proceeds to charities in the city.

3010 20th Street, 94110
+1 415 471 2999
trickdogbar.com

⑤
The Interval, Marina District
Cocktail o'clock

The Interval is a bar, café,
museum, library and home to
the future-focused Long Now
Foundation. Floor-to-ceiling
shelves feature pretty much all
the books needed to restart
civilisation and its centrepiece
is a mechanical prototype of a
10,000-year-old clock.

The bar recreates lost cocktails
from various moments in time
such as the Decanted Mother-in-
Law, a bourbon-based drink served
in a frosty apothecary bottle.
Fort Mason Center Building A,
2 Marina Boulevard, 94123
+1 415 496 9187
theinterval.org

⑥
Toronado Pub, Lower Haight
Landmark beer bar

This Lower Haight establishment is
a grungy, loud and crowded beer-
lover's dream. It's known for surly
bartenders and a rotating selection
of 100-plus craft beers. The most
notable is Pliny the Elder, an
Imperial IPA of cultish renown
brewed by the Santa Rosa-based
Russian River Brewing Company.
This is the only place in San
Francisco where it's always on tap.

But be advised, there's no
kitchen here. Instead, you're
encouraged to bring a sausage
from Rosamunde Sausage Grill
next door.
547 Haight Street, 94117
+1 415 863 2276
toronado.com

Retail
—— Spending time

The connection between shop and maker is strong in this foggiest of cities – in fact, there's often no divide between the two. It's normal to see (or hear) a team somewhere behind the till busying themselves designing, stitching or sanding the very products for sale on the shelves. It's also encouragingly common for proprietors to favour the brands of their Bay Area friends and family, in turn fostering a thriving creative community and begetting a truly distinct and interesting offering.

We must warn you, however: this slow approach to consumerism and value in quality materials means that prices – even for the simplest of cotton tees – are at a premium, much like most things across the city. But steel yourself, because our tour of San Francisco's top retailers will make it near impossible for you to resist at least a little retail therapy.

① Welcome Stranger, Hayes Valley
Functional classics

Catherine Chow and Corina Nurimba own three shops in Hayes Valley; this is the standout. Every collection here is simple, classic and functional. "We're constantly on the go, whether at the beach, in the city or in between, so anything that isn't wearable wouldn't make sense for our brand," says Chow.

Everything by the in-house label is made in San Francisco from fabrics sourced in Japan and Italy. There are also ceramics, independent magazines, grooming products and pieces from brands such as APC and Saturdays NYC.
460 Gough Street, 94102
+1 415 864 2079
welcomestranger.com

2
Tanner Goods, Nopa
Leather forecast

Leather brand Tanner Goods, based in Portland, Oregon, was founded in 2006 and opened its San Francisco flagship in 2015. All of its hard-wearing burnished leather items – from belts and wallets to bags and dog accessories – bear the "Made in USA" stamp and are designed, cut and stitched in the company's Portland workshop.

The range is available in various vegetable-dye finishes and is on display here alongside collaborative projects such as clothing made with Pendleton Woolen Mills and shoes by venerated bootmaker Danner.

651 Divisadero Street, 94117
+ 1 415 757 0614
tannergoods.com

A different collar for every day of the week!

3
Taylor Stitch, Mission District
Don an Oxford

In 2008, friends Michael Armenta, Michael Maher and Barrett Purdum created a modern take on the Oxford shirt: an alternative to existing stuffy button-ups. This founding item still pulls a crowd to their flagship, where staff will happily scale a ladder to grab you shirts from cubbyhole shelves.

The in-house denim is cut and sewn in San Francisco, while the chinos and dress shirts are produced by a Portuguese manufacturer. The brand's second shop in the Marina District also carries its womenswear line.

383 Valencia Street, 94103
+ 1 415 621 2231
taylorstitch.com

4
Unionmade, The Castro
Stateside selection

Like its sister location Mill (*see page 50*), you have to seek out Unionmade. It's just off Valencia Street in a pre-1906 house and fills two large rooms with a dapper selection of menswear, accessories and grooming products.

The clothes lean towards (but are not limited to) an all-American bent, with the Levi's Vintage range, Golden Bear outerwear and Unionmade's own line of patterned bandanas and classic T-shirts. The smart fit-out, sweeping selection of goods and friendly service make it a favourite among San Franciscans.

493 Sanchez Street, 94114
+ 1 415 861 3373
unionmadegoods.com

(5)

Self Edge, Mission District
East meets west

The story goes that husband and wife Kiya and Demitra Babzani founded this petite vault of denim in 2006 after finding Japanese brands making American-style vintage denim better than their US counterparts; they simply imported the best examples and set up shop.

They're still in the same location, selling the same 15 core denim brands that they started with (mostly men's, with a small selection of women's) but have extended their reach to Los Angeles, New York, Portland, Oregon and San José del Cabo.
714 Valencia Street, 94110
+1 415 558 0658
selfedge.com

Go for Gold

Casual Californian menswear label Benny Gold was once just a side project for its graphic-designer namesake. Now it's a respected streetwear line known for its paper-plane motifs and collaborations with brands such as JanSport and Los Angeles-based CLSC.
bennygold.com

1

Al's Attire, North Beach
Clothed from top to bottom

Roped into wardrobe production for a local musical, shoemaker Al Ribaya (*pictured*) taught himself how to dress the theatre troupe from head to toe. By 1979 he had opened his first shop.

Today his North Beach site is cluttered with mannequins, denim jackets and Ribaya's made-to-order leather boots: he and his team still use wooden lasts whittled to the shape of each customer's foot. "Timelessness is all in the construction," says Ribaya, who can often be found at the large workbench next to the window.
1300 Grant Avenue, 94133
+1 415 693 9900
alsattire.com

②
45R, Lower Pacific Heights
Orient express

Riding the popular wave of relaxed Californian meets tailored Japanese, Tokyo-based 45R opened here in 2016. Up the hill from Japantown, the wood-panelled shop stocks the brand's Japanese blue-and-indigo-dyed men's and womenswear, highlights of which are their loose-fitting linen jackets and printed scarves. The garments are made from silks, cottons and denims.

When you're finished here, head across the road to Narumi, where owner Jiro Nakamura has been selling silk kimonos for more than three decades.
1905 Fillmore Street, 94115
+1 415 359 0045
sf45r.com

③
Modern Appealing Clothing, Hayes Valley
Unique offering

Siblings Chris (*pictured*) and Ben Ospital founded Modern Appealing Clothing (Mac) in the 1980s. The duo fill their racks with domestic and international collections from offbeat designers such as Dries Van Noten, Andrea Cammarosano and San Francisco-based Evelyn Muir.

"We try to buy small collections from designers doing interesting things, both in our backyard and further afield," says Chris. The siblings opened a second location in Dogpatch in 2011.
387 Grove Street, 94102
+1 415 863 3011
modernappealingclothing.com

Acrimony, Hayes Valley
Split from the norm

Jenny Chung, the owner of Scandi-inspired Acrimony, travels regularly to discover new labels to add to her bold and constantly evolving collection.

While there are statement pieces for both men and women, Chung values a sturdy staple and tempers her stock with practical shoes and basics. She's always rotating brands but you can count on finding pieces by Henrik Vibskov, Redone and Rachel Comey.
Suite 100, 333 Hayes Street, 94102
+1 415 861 1025
shopacrimony.com

④
Mollusk Surf Shop, Outer Sunset
Laidback appeal

Mollusk Surf Shop oozes sun-bleached 1970s nostalgia. Husband-and-wife artists John McCambridge and Johanna St Clair started the surf, art and clothing brand in 2005, inspired by the DIY art culture of the city in the 1990s.

The shop's cheery interiors are courtesy of fellow Outer Sunset resident Jay Nelson, the walls feature prints for sale and there's a stellar collection of photographers' books dotting the shelves. The highlight is the super-soft tees with wistful Californian surf motifs for both kids and grown-ups.
4500 Irving Street, 94122
+1 415 564 6300
mollusksurfshop.com

Vintage threads

A few former big names in the vintage trade may have diluted their offerings of late but Decades of Fashion in the Haight is still worth visiting for its prohibition glamour, as is Vacation in the Tenderloin for its 1970s and 1980s garb.
decadesoffashionsf.com;
vacation-sf.com

Ⓖ
The Voyager Shop, Mission District
Ethical and exciting

Clothing shop Revolver in the Lower Haight was the launch pad for Marta Fernandez (*pictured*) and Valerie Hirsch, who later went on to found The Voyager Shop. Here you'll find everything from fashion to homeware.

Fernandez now looks after the shop on Valencia and Hirsch is down in Los Angeles at their second outpost. The duo select designers who excite them and who have ethical business models, resulting in a collection from the likes of First Rite, Waltz and Baggu.

365 Valencia Street, 94103
+1 213 995 9951
thevoyagershop.com

Ⓐ
Hero Shop, Tenderloin
Paragon pieces

After 12 years in New York, a hefty slice of which was spent as an editor at *Vogue*, Emily Holt moved home to launch bricks-and-mortar womenswear outpost Hero Shop.

"San Francisco felt like the right place," says Holt. "I think it has a stronger sense of style and interest in fashion than it's given credit for." Her polished shop up the hill in the Tenderloin stocks a rousing and colourful range of international favourites, as well as plenty of local heroes. "There's great talent here that deserves to be on the same stage as bigger brands," she says.

982 Post Street, 94109
+1 415 829 3129
heroshopsf.com

②
Mill, Noe Valley
Easy style

The women's counterpart to menswear shop Unionmade (*see page 45*), Mill exemplifies Californian effortlessness: think white and indigo linens, smartly tailored denim and soft leather sandals and bags.

The extensive multibrand collection (more than 80 at last count) flows seamlessly between the best from New York-based Caron Callahan and San Francisco brand Umber & Ochre, through to Bryr Studio clogs, Aesop skincare and Hasami Porcelain Japan homeware.
*3751 24th Street, 94114
+1 415 401 8920
millmercantile.com*

③
Freda Salvador, Pacific Heights
Amazing feet

Everyday wear with interesting details is the idea behind Megan Papay and Cristina Palomo-Nelson's shoe label for women. El Salvadorian by birth, Palomo-Nelson is from a shoemaking family and met Papay while working for a Bay Area designer.

Their shoes are made in a small family-run factory in Spain, while collaborations with other San Francisco residents such as modernist artist Clare Rojas and jewellery designer Sarah Swell help boost the mules, brogues and boots from season to season.
*2416 Fillmore Street, 94115
+1 415 872 9690
fredasalvador.com*

④
Anaïse, Mission District
A touch of romance

For womenswear, Anaïse's edit of the usual suspects is one of the most interesting in the city. The feminine yet fearless selection favours romantic ready-to-wear collections reminiscent of 1960s French cinema and comes from the likes of New York's A Détacher and Paris's Wanda Nylon.

Former pharmacist Renee Friedrich opened this shop in 2015 and fitted it with mid-century Italian lamps and a Mies van der Rohe Barcelona chair to perfectly accompany her cracking collection and creative visual merchandising.
*3686 20th Street, 94110
+1 408 807 9379
shopanaise.com*

①
General Store, Outer Sunset
California cool

Serena Mitnik-Miller and Mason St Peter (an artist and architect respectively) opened this design concept store in 2009. Its popularity singlehandedly enticed San Franciscans out of the city centre and west to the Outer Sunset, prompting the opening of a second location in Venice Beach in 2012.

The round-up of homeware, stationery, accessories and clothing best represents classic Californian cool and is sourced from a host of talented small-scale makers such as city-based designers Luke Bartels, Julie Cloutier and Nu Swim.
4035 Judah Street, 94122
+ 1 415 682 0600
shop-generalstore.com

⑤
Gravel & Gold, Mission District
Independent women

This proudly all-female independent label is well-known for its fabric print featuring voluptuous – ahem – melons but its scope is far more robust; the brand commissions original art for its in-house line of clothing, with new collections several times a year.

This ethos of fostering a broad network of artists and makers flows down to its production in workshops and factories within the city limits. As well as its own label, Gravel & Gold stocks jewellery, prints and pottery, most of which is by Californian designers.
3266 21st Street, 94110
+ 1 415 552 0112
gravelandgold.com

2

Workshop Residence, Dogpatch
Designed on site

Some questioned Ann Hatch's sanity when she opened this artist space-cum-shop in the industrial Dogpatch back in 2011. "I have a certain reputation for thinking in slightly unconventional ways," says Hatch (*pictured*), whose family is steeped in art patronage (at age 11 she was sipping brandy with Salvador Dali). "Dogpatch seemed an unpretentious, rustic area and manufacturing already existed here."

Her aim to foster artistic talent through a for-profit model was realised in 2011 when she began selling wares by rotating designers. Cast-iron cooking pots by Gay Outlaw and Bob Schmitz, mosaic textiles by graphic designer Jennifer Morla and tessellated dustpans by Hannah Quinn are just a few of the handsome products available in the lofty space.
833 22nd Street, 94107
+1 415 285 2050
workshopresidence.com

③
Wingtip, Financial District
Male order shopping

Ami Arad left the world of software to open his ideal one-stop shop, where he could find a tailored suit, the best bourbon and accessories for his next fly-fishing trip.

Housed in an old bank, it may sound like an unusual mix but the execution is sharp. Luxury brands Alfred Dunhill, St James of London and Agave Denim are staples, as are the finest imported Japanese whiskies and Italian pewter and crystal barware. Arad has also opened a wine cellar in the former vault and a private club on the top floor.
550 Montgomery Street, 94111
+1 415 765 0993
store.wingtip.com

Homeware
Domestic bliss

①
Heath Ceramics, Mission District
All in one

This homeware brand, founded by Edith Heath in 1948, was bought by Robin Petravic and Catherine Bailey in 2003. Following intelligent expansion, they transferred their tile production to the Mission, where they also opened a retail space.

Besides a homeware collection, the site has a kitchen for demonstrations, work stations for custom orders, a newsstand and a coffee cart. Plus, just around the corner the Heath-run Boiler Room hosts pop-up shops, events and exhibitions.
2900 18th Street, 94110
+1 415 361 5552
heathceramics.com

01 Harrington Galleries,
Mission District: Founded
in 1966, this venerated
two-floor emporium on
Valencia Street offers
everything from beds to
tables, artwork and the
odd arcade game.
harringtongalleries.com

02 De Angelis, Mission
District: A few doors
down from Harrington
Galleries, De Angelis
offers a refined selection
of mid-century furniture,
mainly from Denmark.
+1 415 861 9800

03 Another Time, Hayes
Valley: A little rough
around the edges, this
shop stocks chairs, desks
and more from art deco
to mid-century.
anothertimesf.com

04 Big Daddy's Antiques,
Potrero Hill: The extensive
inventory here spans many
decades and is kept in
shape by in-house
woodworkers, welders
and experienced restorers.
bdantiques.com

05 Stuff, Mission District:
This multi-level ode to all
things vintage carries not
just furniture but also
clothes, homeware and
even retro San Francisco-
themed trinkets.
stuffsf.com

②
Flora Grubb Gardens, Bayview
Growth industry

If you have any semblance of
a green thumb, you should visit
Flora Grubb Gardens. Aptly
named co-founder and landscape
designer Flora Grubb has created
an impressive gardening centre
where the dry Californian climate
informs a stock of drought-
resistant greenery, styled in
imaginative arrangements.

If you want to take home more
than ideas, Californian-made pots,
gardening tools and seeds are
available. Ritual Coffee Roasters
also has a kiosk inside, an ideal
excuse to linger among the foliage.
1634 Jerrold Avenue, 94124
+1 415 626 7256
floragrubb.com

Name of the game
———
Since its inception in 1999,
Jay Jeffers' eponymous
interior design studio has built
a loyal following not only in
the Bay Area but nationwide.
For a window into Jeffers'
opulent taste, visit his
shop on Post Street.
jayjeffers-thestore.com

③

Acacia, Mission District
Handmade craftsmanship

Like many independent San Francisco retailers, lawyer Lily Chau (*pictured*) left a demanding desk job to start something new. Her plan: to open a design savvy homeware shop, despite having no design or retail experience.

"Acacia started as an experiment of sorts," says Chau, who opened in 2012 with a focus on Bay Area talent and small-run production. "Handmade goods are diminishing in a society where mass-production is the norm, so people value all the more the distinctive work of each craftsperson and designer."
415 Valencia Street, 94103
+1 415 643 4847
acaciasf.com

④

March, Pacific Heights
Kitchen classics

Sam Hamilton moved to San Francisco after 12 years in marketing and design with Ralph Lauren in New York; she opened March in 2003 as a design shop and today it has a kitchen focus.

Often specially commissioned, items include Agas and US-made cast-iron pans, mugs by a Tuscan potter and vintage dishes by Beatrice Wood. "I love feeling like you're living with heirlooms," says Hamilton. "I want my kids to say, 'Mum, we don't want you to die anytime soon but when you do we want your kitchen canisters'."
3075 Sacramento Street, 94115
+1 415 931 7433
marchsf.com

⑤

The Future Perfect, Pacific Heights
Statement pieces

The Future Perfect started out in New York in 2003 before opening in San Francisco a decade later. Owner David Alhadeff positions the shop as a gallery, exhibiting limited-edition and often one-off pieces such as Lindsey Adelman lighting, Jason Miller ceramics and Piet Hein Eek furniture.

The exclusive showroom on a hilly Pacific Heights' residential street is next door to March and while the steep price tags may not allow you to fill your living room, it's a great place to source a headlining piece.
3085 Sacramento Street, 94115
+1 415 932 6508
thefutureperfect.com

⑥
Woodshop, Outer Sunset
Go with the grain

On a buzzing stretch of Noriega
in the Outer Sunset is a high-
ceilinged space housing artists and
designers. This workshop with a
showroom is shared by sign-painter
and artist Jeff Canham, surfboard-
maker Danny Hess, furniture
designer Luke Bartels (*pictured,
left*) and chair designer Josh Duthie
(*pictured, right*).

As its name suggests, all four
designers work with a mix of
salvaged and harvested woods
such as elm, bay laurel and walnut
to produce a fetching offering of
chopping boards, stools, safari
chairs and longboards.
*3725 Noriega Street, 94122
woodshopsf.com*

①
The Aesthetic Union,
Mission District
Press gang

This petite shopfront in the same
industrial block as Heath Ceramics
(*see page 53*) is the client-facing
side of James Tucker's (*pictured*)
rather traditional printing press.
It's stocked with in-house prints,
as well as other San Francisco
products such as watercolours
by Case for Making and Triangle
House notebooks.

All of the brand's print work
takes place just behind the shop
using Tucker's suite of time-
honoured machines such as a
1931 Vandercook proof press and
a 1952 Heidelberg cylinder press.
*555 Alabama Street, 94110
theaestheticunion.com*

Three more makers

01 Odsy Workshop, Parkside: Seeking a studio for their leatherwork, husband and wife Soojin Chae and Yina Kim found a shoe-repair shop on the western outskirts of town. Before the previous owner left, however, he trained them in his trade and today the couple fix footwear as well as offer wallets and bags.
odsyworkshop.com

02 Small Trade Company, Mission District: Matt Dick's penchant for design took him to Japan for an apprenticeship as an indigo dyer, before he returned here for eight years at multidisciplinary studio Tamotsu Yagi Design. He now runs his own company and designs everything from bags to workwear.
smalltradecompany.com

03 The Thing Quarterly, Tenderloin: *The Thing Quarterly* is an artist-run, object-based publication, with each issue formulated by a different contributor. Alongside the magazine, the eponymous shop offers unique products made by its artists.
thethingquarterly.com

Knife's edge

While it hasn't attempted to make its own in-house range, knife shop Bernal Cutlery stocks a comprehensive selection of French, Japanese, US and vintage blades. It also offers professional sharpening on a Japanese whetstone and workshops on knife skills.
bernalcutlery.com

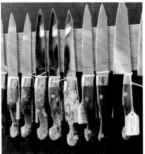

(2)
Town Cutler, Lower Nob Hill
Blade runner

At the age of five, Galen Garretson received his first pocket knife and although it resulted in him needing six stitches in his head, it began an obsession that would see him leave his sous-chef job at Quince and open Town Cutler.

He started small, selling Japanese and US-made kitchen blades, before slowly adding his own range of scabbards, bags and finally knives. His inventory is made from US carbon steel and Swedish stainless steel in a range of unique forms and every piece is shaped and sharpened in store.
1005 Bush Street, 94109
+1 415 359 1519
towncutler.com

(3)
In Fiore, Lower Nob Hill
Skincare specialist

Apothecary Julie Elliott employs a herbal approach in the creation of her skincare range and formulates body balms, toners, serums and fragrances from plant products and essential oils such as Napa-grown grapeseed oil.

All of the own-label products are manufactured in the Bay Area, while the workshop above the Lower Nob Hill premises looks after the packaging. As well as its own extensive selection, the wood-panelled shop is one of the only places outside Japan that stocks the brand's anti-ageing collaboration with Albion Cosmetics.
868 Post Street, 94109
infiore.net

④
Joshu+Vela, Mission District
Bag yourself a classic

Visit this whitewashed Mission
space and you'll hear the whirr of
the pedal sewing machines and the
hammer of the leather workers out
back as they create owner Noah
Guy's (*pictured, left*) collection of
totes, backpacks and duffels.

Every item in the shop adheres
to Guy's preferred raw-canvas
and rough-leather look and, what's
more, everything is built to last.
It's entirely possible that this
penchant for visible durability is a
result of Guy's years as a designer
at labels such as The North Face
and Levi's.
3042 16th Street, 94103
+1 415 872 5347
joshuvela.com

⑤
Ampersand, Mission District
Flower power

This florist is brimming with
Californian natives and unique
and unusual foliage sourced from
nearby farms by owners and
husbands Emerson Boyle and
Benjamin Boso. "We don't use
flower fridges and we try to find
weird species that aren't your
average flower," says Boyle. "We
like that people can come and
explore things they've never seen."

Pick up one of the fresh and
constantly rotating bouquets or opt
for a Californian souvenir: cedar,
juniper or blue sage dried in-house
and tied into an incense bundle.
80 Albion Street, 94103
+1 415 654 0776
ampersandsf.com

La bella vita

One block from Market Street
is three-decade-old stalwart of
the city retail scene, Bell'occhio
("beautiful eye" in Italian).
Owner Claudia Schwartz's mix
of new and vintage ribbons,
letter sets, craft tools and
other worldly curiosities has a
wholesome 1950s bent.
bellocchio.com

*Ok, got the flowers.
Now, who's the
lucky lady...*

⑥
Schein & Schein, North Beach
Top of the charts

Although husband and wife Jimmie
and Marti Schein started out in the
music business, they have always
been resourceful collectors. This
cosy wood-panelled shop dedicated
to vintage maps is something of
a natural venture for them, then,
given that they've amassed a
collection of about 7,500.

Opened in 2003, the shop
catalogues cartography from the
14th to the 20th centuries. The
plethora of rare and intricate maps
of the Bay Area and surrounding
wine regions has mostly been
obtained from university libraries
(after the originals have been
digitised), as well as via local
donations and estate collections.
If the older originals take your
fancy but the price tag is a little
out of reach, you can enquire about
a printed copy.
1435 Grant Avenue, 94133
+1 415 399 8882
scheinandschein.com

Books and records
Stop, look, listen

①
Green Apple Books,
Inner Richmond
Pick of the reads

This bookshop, housed in a rickety
pre-1906 building, was founded
by former soldier and airline
radio technician Richard Savoy
in 1967. Its collection of new and
secondhand volumes includes
cooking and fiction sections near
the register, children's books at the
back and photography, architecture,
poetry and US socialism upstairs.

As well as the main shop, there's
a fiction and music annexe a few
doors down and a second location
on the southern edge of Golden
Gate Park.

506 Clement Street, 94118
+1 415 387 2272
greenapplebooks.com

②
City Lights, North Beach
On the literary Beat

Sociology professor Peter D Martin
founded rebellious magazine *City
Lights* in 1952 and also opened
the country's first all-paperback
bookshop in collaboration with
Beat poet Lawrence Ferlinghetti.

In 1955, Ferlinghetti bought
Martin's share of the business for
$1,000 and that same year began
publishing titles, perhaps the most
famous of which remains Allen
Ginsberg's controversial *Howl and
Other Poems*. Today the three-level
maze of books remains one of
the most prominent and storied
bookshops in the US.

261 Columbus Avenue, 94133
+1 415 362 8193
citylights.com

④
Stranded, Mission District
New age for Aquarius

Many San Franciscans are still in mourning over the 2016 closure of the city's oldest independent music shop, Aquarius Records. Dating back to 1970, it stocked unusual and rare releases, garnering a loyal gang of indie rock groupies.

The good news is Oakland-based shop Stranded has taken over the skinny premises, as well as Aquarius's longstanding dedication to both old and new independent talent. Stranded has also brought its own identity to the mix, stocking vinyl from artists on its in-house label, Superior Viaduct.
1055 Valencia Street, 94110
+1 415 647 2272
strandedrecords.com

③
Amoeba Music, Haight-Ashbury
Wide-ranging catalogue

Much like its home neighbourhood of the Haight-Ashbury, Amoeba wears its anti-establishment disposition on its sleeve. From obscure releases to the top 40, its focus is on stocking the broadest possible range of music.

It started out in 1990 in a small shop in Berkeley, before opening a second space across the bay in 1997 and a third site in Los Angeles in 2001. All this time, the eminent name in discography has remained fiercely independent and continues to attract impressive names to perform in store.
1855 Haight Street, 94117
+1 415 831 1200
amoeba.com

Things we'd buy
—— Take-home treats

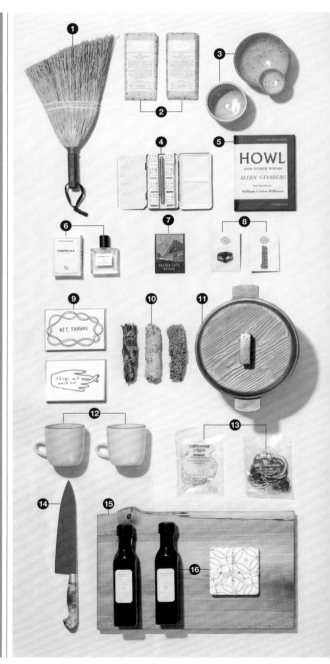

There's a lot being created in San Francisco's tucked-away studio spaces, with makers and designers turning out all manner of products that dominate the shelves of the city's independently owned outposts. In fact, it's almost impossible to walk away from one of these shops without a purchase or two.

Whether it's tableware from the venerated Heath Ceramics, titles by history's most famed Beat poets (published in-house at City Lights) or the latest Californian fashion from young design houses Taylor Stitch, Freda Salvador and Nu Swim, there's plenty of opportunity to give your credit card a workout.

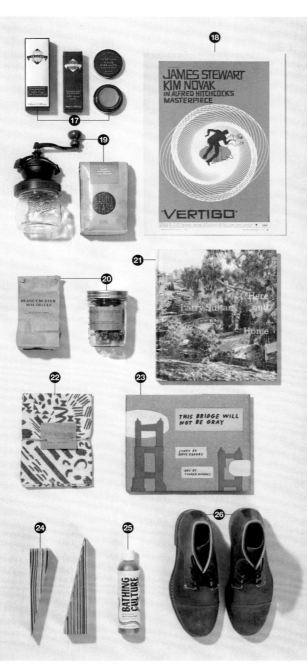

01 Hannah Quinn broom from Workshop Residence
workshopresidence.com
02 Dandelion chocolate
dandelionchocolate.com
03 Julie Cloutier ceramics from General Store
shop-generalstore.com
04 Watercolours by Case for Making *caseformaking.com*
05 *Howl and Other Poems* by Allen Ginsberg from City Lights
citylights.com
06 Bruno Fazzolari fragrances from Workshop Residence
workshopresidence.com
07 Golden Gate Bridge magnet from Aggregate Supply
aggregatesupplysf.com
08 PSA San Francisco badges from The Voyager Shop
thevoyagershop.com
09 People I've Loved cards from General Store
shop-generalstore.com
10 Incense bundles by Ampersand *ampersandsf.com*
11 Gay Outlaw and Bob Schmitz cast-iron pot from Workshop Residence
workshopresidence.com
12 Mugs by Heath Ceramics
heathceramics.com
13 Dardimans fruit crisps from Foodhall *foodhallsf.com*
14 Chef's knife by Town Cutler
towncutler.com
15 Luke Bartels chopping board from Woodshop
woodshopsf.com
16 Olive oil, balsamic vinegar and tableware by March
marchsf.com
17 Skincare by In Fiore
infiore.net
18 *Vertigo* film poster from SFMoma Museum Store
museumstore.sfmoma.org
19 Camano coffee mill and beans from Sightglass Coffee
sightglasscoffee.com
20 Peanut butter maltballs and brittle from Mr and Mrs Miscellaneous
+1 415 970 0750
21 *Here and Home* by Larry Sultan from Green Apple Books
greenapplebooks.com
22 Jenny Pennywood tea towel from General Store
shop-generalstore.com

23 *This Bridge Will Not Be Gray* by Dave Eggers from Aggregate Supply *aggregatesupplysf.com*
24 Nick Pourfard and Michael Svendsen doorstops from Workshop Residence *workshopresidence.com*
25 Bathing Culture bubble bath from General Store *shop-generalstore.com*
26 Al Ribaya boots from Al's Attire *alsattire.com*

27 Nu Swim bikini from General Store *shop-generalstore.com*
28 Cap and socks by Benny Gold *bennygold.com*
29 Men's Oxford shirt by Taylor Stitch *taylorstitch.com*
30 Duffel bag by Joshu+Vela *joshuvela.com*
31 Women's shoes by Freda Salvador *fredasalvador.com*

12 essays
San Francisco stories

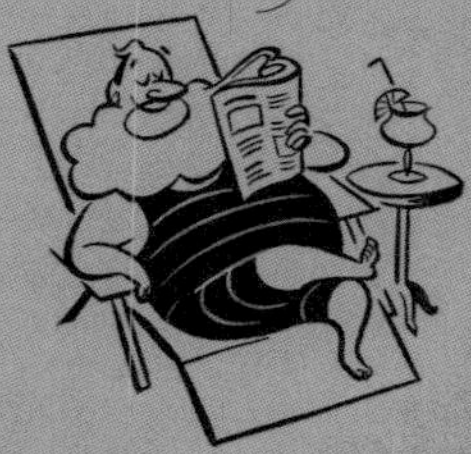

Keeping you at Bay
Natural attractions

———

The landscape of San Francisco and the Bay Area weaves a subtle yet compelling enchantment that wins over even the most sceptical resident.

by Mallory Farrugia, writer

I never imagined that I would live in San Francisco. I never cared too much for the Beats, never fantasised about family life in the Painted Ladies, never felt wooed by Silicon Valley's futuristic promises. Besides, I love sunshine. But after stints in Los Angeles and New York, I found myself bound for northern California in 2013, when the technology economy was beginning its second meteoric upswing and my husband had received a job offer that couldn't be refused.

That was also the first drought year – and throughout the summer of 2013 the legendary San Francisco fog was nowhere to be seen. The days were balmy enough to spend at the beach, a pastime that most residents wilfully dismiss because it's rarely warm enough to sit on the sand without a sweater. I remember first discovering Ocean Beach and its beauty – unparalleled as far as city beaches go. With its deep shade of cyan and dozens of wetsuit-clad surfers gracefully riding sets

of head-and-a-half-high waves, the water lulls you into thinking that you're somewhere much closer to the equator. I'd been warned that the water was colder than I could imagine but I stubbornly ignored the friendly advice as I drove west one particularly hot Saturday. At the edge of the water I stripped off and ran in but only got about knee-deep before bailing out, crestfallen. It was freezing.

Having this crystal-clear but unbearably icy water on my doorstep taunted me for another year or so, until a truly sweltering heatwave set in. Due to the temperate climate, most apartments and homes in San Francisco don't have air-conditioning, so there was no respite to be found except in the water. I finally went in. And when I came out, I was changed. Going underwater at Ocean Beach is a complete and utter shock to the system. It jolts you into the present moment. It wipes out language and coherent thought. Submerged, you can't feel anything except the cold. But when you come out and lie down on the sand, soaking wet and giddy, you're awake to everything.

"I started noticing the way the ocean smells. It's an integral part of northern California's unmistakable perfume"

After that, I started noticing the way the ocean smells. It's an integral part of northern California's unmistakable perfume: a blend of salt water, eucalyptus, lavender and the *Helichrysum splendidum* shrub. I took to walking the trail called Land's End – an apt name, because it feels like the edge of the world – where that scent floats on the wind, mixing with the woodsy smell of cypress and pine trees as you head around the northern edge of the Presidio.

As autumn set in, I wanted to surround myself with the smell of trees, so I ventured out to Muir Woods (*see page 135*), a redwood preserve about 45 minutes north of the city. To get there, you drive over the Golden Gate Bridge, along the Panoramic Highway, which looks out over the Marin Headlands, and then down a winding canyon road until you reach the forest. The preserve encompasses some 558 hectares, just under half of which is home to old-growth coast redwoods, most of them 600 to 800 years old. I'd never stood in the presence of a redwood tree before, let alone in the middle of a small forest. Take just a few steps into their shade and it's as if you've entered an ancient cathedral. The temperature drops noticeably and the air smells like a mix of mountains and ocean. As for the silence, it envelops you.

In pursuit of an even more remote retreat, I began to explore the Sonoma Coast. Friends recommended places such as Point Reyes and Jenner but the destination that captured my imagination was Sea Ranch, a planned community with strict architectural guidelines to ensure that the structures built within its boundaries blend in with the craggy coastline. Situated on a slim 16km stretch of land that runs between the ocean and the mountains, the "town" is home to fewer than 2,000 homes, only a fraction of which are inhabited all year round. A 19-room lodge hosts overnight guests and doubles as the only post office and restaurant with dinner service for some distance.

According to the map, it's about three hours north of San Francisco but in reality it's more like five – not because of traffic but because of the road you have to take to get there. The narrow cliffside route is bordered by a vertical drop to the ocean on one side and a forested mountainside on the other, with hairpin turns that are not for the faint-hearted. You might see sheep sleeping on the cliffs or cows grazing on the mountainside but the only evidence of human civilisation is the paved road beneath your tyres. When you arrive, there's no mobile-phone service, no Tesla charging station, no place to buy snacks. The landscape is a blend of three earthy colours: blue ocean and sky; green grass and foliage; and brown wood. When night falls, you have an unfettered view of the cosmos. Part of the community's design entailed strict regulation of outdoor lighting, including a ban on streetlights.

Back in San Francisco and with winter in full swing, my local wine shop held a special tasting of Sonoma Coast reds. Most of the winemakers were there, chatting with customers and tasting other wines themselves. The final wine on the docket – spider chase – came from Cazadero, a town of fewer than 500 people just southeast of Sea Ranch. As I ruminated on the name, the winemakers came over to my table as if on cue and explained it to me. During harvest season they would walk through the vineyard in the early mornings, when the hillside was still shrouded in fog, and watch tiny spiders scurrying out of the way of their footsteps and back onto the vines.

As I tasted the wine, I could imagine the entire scene: the morning silence, the herbal smell, the cool fog and the stunning view from the hilltop to the ocean that would be revealed when it burned off. And that's when I knew: this was my terroir. — (M)

ABOUT THE WRITER: Mallory Farrugia is a writer, producer and book editor, living in the Outer Richmond in San Francisco.

ESSAY 02

A feeling of *Vertigo*
Hitchcock's San Francisco

———

While the city has been the location for any number of films, it was Alfred Hitchcock's sense of place that led to its signature classic.

*by Ben Rylan,
Monocle*

Perched precariously at the edge of a sea wall in the shadow of the Golden Gate Bridge, Fort Point on Marine Drive offers possibly the finest vantage spot from which to absorb the enormous scale of the structure.

Even if you haven't visited Fort Point, however, you may still feel as though you have. Much like the park bench in the shadow of New York's Queensboro Bridge, as seen in Woody Allen's *Manhattan* (1979), this urban patch has popped up in various popular-culture incarnations. Most notably, it was here that the confused Madeleine, as played by Kim Novak, took a fall into the crashing waters of San Francisco Bay, prompting an urgent rescue by James Stewart's Scottie in Alfred Hitchcock's 1958 masterpiece *Vertigo*.

Before Hitchcock began exploring the city's dark side, other film-makers toiling away in the B-movie noir genre of the 1940s had been casting San Francisco as the backdrop to their stories of shadows and mystery. Lauren Bacall helps a wrongly accused Humphrey Bogart sneak past a city roadblock in 1947's *Dark Passage* (before Agnes Moorehead takes a terrifying plunge from the window of an apartment block). And 1950's *Woman on the Run* pulls off a role-reversal by pitting Ann Sheridan in a midnight race across the city to clear her husband's name, culminating in a scream-inducing finale atop a rollercoaster.

Hitchcock had spent time working in various capacities in Europe's mighty silent-era film industry. In the early 1920s, German expressionism was emerging at the forefront of the continent's more sophisticated cinematic exports (even US audiences favoured German films to their tatty homegrown product for much of the pre-talking era) and an encounter with the great film-maker FW Murnau at Germany's Studio Babelsberg piqued Hitchcock's interest in the magic of architecture in movies.

It's fitting then that, of all the locations Hitchcock explored on screen, San Francisco should fuel his particular breed of fascination. The streets are steep, the houses tall and the skyline often cloaked in that atmospheric fog – an attractive phenomenon for a filmmaker who introduced audiences to his preferred themes of mystery and innocence in 1927's *The Lodger: A Story of the London Fog*.

SF post-Hitchcock
——
01 **Bullitt (1968)**
Steve McQueen thriller famed for its iconic car chase.
02 **Dirty Harry (1971)**
Clint Eastwood's cop finds out if SF's criminals are feeling lucky.
03 **Mrs Doubtfire (1993)**
This cross-dressing comedy portrays a gentler image of the city.

From the residential panorama that underpins the plot of *Rear Window* (1954) to the architectural design, inspired by the work of Frank Lloyd Wright, seen in *North By Northwest* (1959), a key aspect of Hitchcock's genius was his ability to turn the built environment into something to be feared. Shortly after title designer Saul Bass's legendary opening sequence introduces us to *Vertigo*, for example, we're dropped, mid-chase, onto the precipitous rooftops of San Francisco's Russian Hill neighbourhood, where Stewart's Scottie narrowly avoids a fatal fall.

Vertiginous anxiety wasn't actually a main thread of the French novel upon which the film is based. Hitchcock himself

"The streets are steep, the houses tall and the skyline often cloaked in that atmospheric fog – an attractive phenomenon for a film-maker"

planted that in his interpretation, dismissing two writers before settling on Sam Taylor, a San Francisco native, to complete the screenplay. The city's geography is used to resonate this thematic addition. The story reveals Novak's Madeleine to be a resident of the Nob Hill neighbourhood, set atop one of the city's original hills, while Scottie's Lombard Street home sits at the foot of a steep descent. To find the woman at the centre of his obsession, he'll quite literally need to climb to dizzying heights.

Like an icy blonde at the centre of a Hitchcock film, San Francisco is aware of its beauty and the way in which it conjures intrigue. If its screen persona is one of mystery, however, the misty peaks of the real city are just as spellbinding and waiting to be investigated. — (M)

ABOUT THE WRITER: Ben Rylan is a producer and presenter for MONOCLE 24 radio and can often be found exploring Hitchcock's film locations, cloaked in a Bogart-inspired trenchcoat.

ESSAY 03

Green streets
San Francisco's parklets

A subversive art installation that turned a car spot into a miniature park was the catalyst for a reclamation of urban spaces that's still going on today.

by Blaine Merker, landscape architect

Forty-Niners, bohemians, Beats, hippies, start-up founders: pick your generation and you'll find someone re-imagining everyday life on the urban canvas of San Francisco. Perhaps it's the city's human scale that gives each brash generation the idea that the streets are theirs for the taking. It's as if it knew that it needed to flatter its latest residents by reflecting their self-styled image back at them, smiling just slightly and taking the effort at urban reinvention with good humour.

Back in 2005 I was just out of grad school and working as a landscape architect. My job was designing parks but just as often I was designing parking lots. Between deadlines I would walk from Union Square to the Financial District to scout locations for an art installation that my friends and I had devised: to re-appropriate a metered parking space and cast it temporarily as a tiny public park.

The project took shape on a sunny autumn day on Mission Street. We fed the meter and obeyed the two-hour limit; back then you could rent 18.5 sq m of this strange urban real estate for $2 an hour, not a bad price for ground-floor property with great foot traffic, and it meant that we were being doubly subversive because we didn't even need to break the law. We unrolled turf on the asphalt, placed a large tree and a bench within the white tick marks and retreated across the street to a roof deck to take pictures.

For the first 10 minutes, nothing. In fact, people assiduously avoided it, no doubt afraid of being suckers for guerrilla marketing. Then one guy took off his shoes and settled onto the cool grass. Right away, someone else – with a pizza – took to the bench. They struck up a conversation. People on the pavement slowed to talk. Bingo.

Our "Park(ing)" installation had been inspired by Gordon Matta-Clark, an artist as young in the 1970s as we were in the 2000s. He had bought "odd lots" around New York at auction, slivers of land that surveying errors had caused to be overlooked, useless for much else other than art. We imagined that a new public commons might emerge through such sites if they could be brought to attention, a kind of countermovement to the relentless commercialisation of space in our crowded, expensive little city. Not long after we posted our images online, the humble parking space caught on as a site of expression and soft rebellion: strangers around the world began riffing on the idea with their own local installations. We created a how-to guide. Park(ing) Day T-shirts and social media followed.

San Francisco remained the crucible for the reimagined pavement and the

"Not long after we posted our images online, the humble parking space caught on as a site of expression and soft rebellion"

contested kerb. By the following year, our one-off installation had become an annual event: Park(ing) Day. Strangers in Berlin and Melbourne sent us photos of their efforts. A same-sex couple wed in a parking space in the Lower Haight, just one example of how local news crews had a field day with human-interest stories. At the same time, we met with interested bureaucrats in the planning department and the mayor's office. Someone unearthed an obscure idea from the city's 1985 plan: small open spaces called "parklets" had been proposed downtown but never implemented. It seemed that these might just be the way to make Park(ing) permanent. The city developed a trial permit system that allowed the tiny park in a parking space to stay.

In a matter of years, San Francisco's parklet programme had created more than 50 semi-permanent installations around the city. Today the waiting list to get a permit is long, with merchant sponsors gladly giving up a parking space to create a place for people to linger on the pavement in this most walkable city. You can find parklets gripping steep streets in Jackson Square, lining Italian cafés along Columbus and strung along the Valencia Street corridor in the Mission District, where they exist in all their delightful density and variety. They appear suddenly in the urban habitat, an indicator species signalling street life on the verge of what real-estate people call "vibrancy".

Parklets have become unlikely portfolio pieces for some of the city's most experimental architects. Local firms such as Boor Bridges, CMG, Ogrydziak Prillinger, Walter Hood and Interstice have left parklet calling cards around San Francisco's neighbourhoods. A novel urban design typology, with a short cycle from design to construction, the parklet offers a tempting venue for emerging designers and fabricators to showcase their talent. Parklets show San Francisco's freaky side in small glimpses: despite the city's libertine reputation its architecture is notoriously fussy, historicist and timid, making the small parklet an opportunity for outsized flair and aesthetic clash.

Critics point to parklets as a potential vector of gentrification, with some neighbourhoods pushing back on new installations. The city responded in 2016 with legislation that assisted in spreading parklets beyond chic corridors to San Francisco's working-class neighbourhoods. (Mamá Art Café at 4754 Mission Street and the Bayview's parklet at 1730 Yosemite Avenue are two examples in outer neighbourhoods.) Dozens of other US cities have followed San Francisco's quixotic example by establishing parklet programmes of their own.

Soon the niche space created by the old-fashioned practice of single private cars in public might disappear entirely. Pedestrians may just walk out into the street, parting a sea of self-driving traffic like Moses, and wonder why those parks were ever built so small. It might be all right if we forget that the reason for these little places for people to gather was originally the antiquated idea that each of us needed to park a car somewhere. — (M)

Three city parklets

01 937 Valencia Street
A succulent garden sponsored by a local homeowner.
02 4033 Judah Street
Reminiscent of a shipwreck, outside Trouble Coffee.
03 2198 Filbert Street
The Rapha Cycling Club's parklet features half a van and a café table.

ABOUT THE WRITER: Blaine Merker is an urbanist, landscape architect and outdoor-loving West Coaster. He directs the office of Gehl in San Francisco and lives just across the bay in Berkeley.

Crafty plans
Design and manufacturing

———

Despite all the big business in the city, it's the smaller artisan crafters and creators who have turned "Made in San Francisco" into a source of pride.

by Hugo Macdonald, writer

Think of design in the context of San Francisco and it's likely that your mind jumps either back in time or forward to the future. Historically the city has given birth to more than its fair share of brands that have shaped modern consumer culture: (The) Gap, Levi's, Banana Republic, North Face and Old Navy, among others. Fast forward to the technology era and the list of companies that call San Francisco home reads like the top 50 of the Fortune 500.

Between big brands and technology, however, is a healthy design sector that often gets overlooked in the starrier story of the city. These small-scale local craft and manufacturing industries are part of the city's charm and a vital component of its lifeblood.

First-time visitors to the city frequently cite these makers, old and new, as among the more surprising discoveries: the hum and thrum that gives the city a softer side. There are 650-odd craft and manufacturing businesses active in San Francisco, turning out everything from the expected chocolates, coffee, fashion and jewellery to the more niche mattresses, utility-ware and heated outdoor furniture. Combined, they employ more than 5,000 workers and generate about $620m annually. From Dogpatch to Sunset, Mission to Noe Valley, you can find thriving craft, industry and retail with a "Made in San Francisco" label.

Much of this renewed energy is thanks to a non-profit called SF Made, founded in 2010 with a mission to preserve, develop and enhance San Francisco's local manufacturing base. It's an organisation that incubates and supports makers by providing education, connecting resources and hosting networking opportunities to learn and share from each other's experiences. One of its greatest achievements, however, has been to bring this side of the city out from behind the garage doors and into the open. Alongside tours of different workshops, it organises an annual SF Made Week (in May) with a packed programme of events aimed at raising the profile of the community in the city.

One of San Francisco's most visible contemporary-design success stories is Heath Ceramics (*see page 53*). Founded in Sausalito by Edith and Brian Heath in 1948, the small-batch ceramic producer found fame through tactile but durable tiles and tableware with an unmistakeably West Coast spirit. As Edith's health declined so did the company's fortunes, until husband-and-wife duo Robin Petravic and Catherine Bailey purchased the company in 2003.

> *"Between big brands and technology is a healthy design sector that often gets overlooked in the starrier story of the city"*

In Heath they spotted the potential to combine design, manufacturing and retail with a sustainable business-minded approach, preserving and extending the legacy of the original studio.

In 2012, Petravic and Bailey moved their tile production into a former industrial laundry building in the heart of San Francisco. They combined the factory with a large retail space that features a florist-cum-newsstand and a restaurant, Tartine Manufactory (*see page 31*). Here, under one roof, you find a microcosm of San Francisco's living, breathing design scene and a platform for the local community

San Francisco inventions
——
01 The jukebox
Debuted in the city's Palais Royale Saloon in 1889.
02 The slot machine
Created by mechanic Charles Fey in the late 19th century.
03 The waterbed
Designed for a university thesis in 1968.

of makers, a handful of whom rent studio space in the building. Ceramics might not make the most practical souvenirs (though the staff at Heath wrap them immaculately) but no trip to the city would be complete without visiting the factory.

San Francisco's local maker-manufacturing scene is more than a nostalgic yearning for simpler times when things were made locally or by hand. It's a crucial connection in the city's narrative between past, present and future. The city built its fame and fortune on its innovative and entrepreneurial prowess; keeping minds, hands and machines working together will ensure a prosperous future too. — (M)

ABOUT THE WRITER: Hugo Macdonald is a writer and consultant living in London. His favourite thing in San Francisco is the Diego Rivera mural at the Art Institute, which has one of the best views over the city. He was MONOCLE design editor from 2010 to 2013.

ESSAY O5
Let there be rock
Geological foundations

—

The rock on which San Francisco has been built has shaped the growth of the city from its earliest days.

by Gary Kamiya,
writer

San Francisco is famous for many things – its bay, bridges, waterfront and lustful embrace of everything that the Puritans who founded this country abhorred (fortunately they landed on the opposite end of the continent). But it also possesses one little-noticed attribute that is essential to its identity: its rocks. Sublimely unexpected, they break through the urban veneer in the strangest places, close-up announcements of the untamed terrain that sets this metropolis apart from all other cities (Rio aside). Once you've learned to look for them, the naked boulders that pop up in every neighbourhood are as thrilling a manifestation of San Francisco's natural splendour as Land's End or Twin Peaks.

San Francisco's history is inextricably bound up with its rocks. In fact, its history was delayed by them. For more than 200 years, from 1565 onwards, Spanish galleons from Manila sailing down the California coast to Mexico missed the narrow opening in the Coast Range now called the Golden Gate because they had been ordered for reasons of safety to keep to the west of the Farallon Islands (jagged crags 42km off the coast).

When settlers did land, the rocks figured in their tales of the city in different ways. In 1777, a party of Spanish soldiers and priests on their way to the just-built Presidio and Mission got lost in a heavy fog in the southernmost part of the city and decided to camp. The next morning they beheld a beautiful valley, which they named Visitacion. Local lore says that they held a mass, using an enormous boulder as their altar; this boulder still stands in a private backyard on Delta Street.

In San Francisco, geology has always been tied in with destiny. When crowds rushed in to the formerly sleepy hamlet of Yerba Buena in 1849, the rocky, steep, sand-covered hills forced them to settle in the small, flat area between the hills and the waterfront. The site of the young city's first exclusive neighbourhood, South Park, was chosen because "it was the only level spot of equal area, free from sand, within the city limits." Only after 1873, when the cable car was invented, were Nob and Russian hills widely settled.

"The naked boulders that pop up in every neighbourhood are as thrilling a manifestation of San Francisco's natural splendour as Land's End"

Some of the city's most famous neighbourhoods have been shaped – literally – by its battles with rocks. The eastern side of Telegraph Hill was carved out in the 19th century by two rogue quarrymen called the Gray brothers, who illegally blasted away at it for decades, sending houses sliding downhill and creating its dramatic, sheer face.

Today the city fills the 119 sq km peninsula between the bay and the Pacific but countless rocks defiantly remain: the underlying terrain is simply too recalcitrant to be blasted away or covered over. Not even the most coveted and stratospherically priced real estate is exempt. On Powell Street, just two blocks from the swanky hotels on California Street atop Nob Hill, stands a fenced-off lot that has been vacant since the days of the Yelamu Indians, the city's first inhabitants. In the centre of the lot is a massive outcropping of greywacke, the rock that makes up the city's central hills. That ancient boulder is as integral to what this city is all about as the cable cars that roll past it.

Rocks are everywhere here. In Bernal Heights, there's a house built atop a five-metre boulder, which peeps out through the building's garage like an unmoveable car. Glen Canyon is a great gash in the geographical centre of the city, its sheer radiolarian chert walls and mighty boulders preventing development more emphatically than any anti-gentrification coalition. From Hunters Point to Seacliff, there are untold numbers of exposed rocks of all sizes, in plain view or hidden away. These wondrous geological gardens have endured for millions of years and will endure long after this fragile city has crumbled back into the earth that it was temporarily built upon. — (M)

ABOUT THE WRITER: Gary Kamiya is the author of *Cool Gray City of Love: 49 Views of San Francisco*. He was a co-founder of *Salon.com* and is currently executive editor of *San Francisco Magazine*.

ESSAY 06
Techno prisoners?
Beyond the digital industry
——

Are the people of San Francisco really withering in the shadow of the city's technology industry?

by Mark Robinson, features editor at 'Wired'

To read accounts of today's San Francisco is to get the impression that this city has been utterly transformed over the past three decades; that it's awash with billions in venture capital, overrun by dotcom gold-seekers, losing its cherished non-conformity and diversity, and utterly unaffordable. That's the portrait anyway.

In my day-to-day life, there's some evidence of truth to that statement. As an editor at *Wired* – the publication founded in 1993 to chronicle the digital revolution in all its culture-shattering glory – I have a front-row seat to the changes sweeping through my city. Outside my office is a stream of Teslas cruising down Third Street, a profusion of co-working spaces and a glut of engineers who favour bedroom slippers and man buns.

But the fixation on these trivial signifiers of technology-driven transformation misses the bigger picture of a city that still revels in its uniqueness, beauty, vibrancy and windswept *joie de vivre*. I experience that splendour almost every morning at the Dolphin Swimming and Boating Club. Founded in 1877, it sits on the edge of the bay like a wood-panelled museum crossed with a social club, complete with hand-built rowboats, locker rooms, a sauna and a weight room with a view of the Golden Gate Bridge.

On any given morning – especially in winter, when the water temperature drops below 10c – you'll find me and 200 other enthusiasts splashing around our protected cove, not a wetsuit to be seen. To say the experience is exhilarating is an understatement. Swimming in that cold water induces a rush of endorphins unlike any pharmaceutical high. It is, quite simply, addictive (I've been a regular at the Dolphin Club for eight years). The members of this briny institution – about 1,600 at last count – constitute a far more representative cross-section of San Francisco than you'll find in the technology-driven neighbourhood where I work. On any given morning, there are firefighters, lawyers, teachers, building contractors, restaurateurs,

professional musicians and (yes) a journalist or two.

But as much as I love my city, I'm also sad that it has become so unaffordable. The costs are truly mind-bending: in the summer of 2017, the median home price in San Francisco hit $1.45m and the median condo cost $1.16m. This is undoubtedly driven by the fact that San Francisco and the entire Bay Area is the beating heart of the technology industry but the picture is much more complicated than that. Technology only represents about 10 per cent of private-sector employment in the city: management, business and financial jobs account for almost 18 per cent of jobs, while office and administrative support gigs represent another 14 per cent. Still, those technology jobs are higher paying than in other industries and their number is growing, meaning that most city residents are being priced out of the housing market.

"San Francisco stubbornly holds on to a free-spirited weirdness that predates the digital revolution by decades"

But San Francisco stubbornly holds on to a free-spirited weirdness that predates the digital revolution by decades. The other night I stopped into the Roxie (*see page 90*) in the Mission District to check out a programme of film clips gleaned from the archives of Oddball Films (more than 50,000 documentaries, home movies and industrial films). The cinema, once a porno house, was packed. And don't get me started about the city's (unofficial) LSD Museum, its eerie wave organ (powered by surf) or its annual Folsom Street Fair (a cheerfully sadomasochistic "leather pride" extravaganza).

So I'm staying in the City by the Bay. Someday I hope to join the group of retirees who gather at the Dolphin Club every afternoon: they call themselves the Old Goats. I'm sure they keep each other young with their teasing, leisurely lunches and unhurried swims. One of them likes to quote the long-time *San Francisco Chronicle* columnist Herb Caen: "One day if I go to heaven... I'll look around and say, 'It ain't bad but it ain't San Francisco.'" — (M)

ⓘ

ABOUT THE WRITER: Mark Robinson is a features editor at *Wired* magazine. He's devoted to open-water swimming and moonlights as a jazz singer. In 2005, he and the writer Jeff Howe coined the word "crowdsourcing".

ESSAY 07
Talking about a revolution
Bay Area counterculture
——
From the disenfranchised to the pushers of society's boundaries, the region has long been a hotbed of activism and clamourings for change.

*by Mikaela Aitken,
Monocle*

There's hardly a decade in the past century when the residents of the Bay Area sat still, content with society's trajectory. Rather, the region's history is flush with gallant protagonists and influential social movements that shaped the political landscape of not just the immediate region but the state, the country and at times the world.

Kicking things off – not necessarily for the Bay Area but for the purpose of this piece – was Clara Elizabeth Chan Lee, who in 1911, at the age of 25, bucked the strict cultural norms of the time and registered to vote in Oakland. Women had just regained the right to vote in California (such rights weren't re-adopted nationwide until 1920) and Lee was the first Chinese-American woman to register in the US. She also encouraged self-reliance through the Chinese Women's Jeloab Association.

Fast forward a few decades to the depths of the Second World War, just after

the attack on Pearl Harbor. In a blatant violation of civil liberties, President Roosevelt signed an executive order that mandated that all Japanese-Americans on the West Coast must enter internment camps. Resisting the order, 23-year-old welder Fred Korematsu went into hiding, only to be arrested in San Leandro a month later. While in jail, Korematsu began a vocal protest against the government's order but lost the case. Nonetheless, his story made news nationwide, amassing growing opposition against Roosevelt. It was also after the Second World War that the US military dishonourably discharged 9,000 gay servicemen and women, most of whom happened to be processed out of service in San Francisco – but we'll come back to that in a moment.

In the late 1940s, dishevelled, chain-smoking literature students who were disenchanted by post-war US began spinning webs of anti-establishment words and by the 1950s they became known as the Beat Generation. These bohemian mavericks descended on North Beach and, although identifying as apolitical, their advocation of personal illumination

"Their advocation of personal illumination through drugs, sex and jazz saw them claim a place on the political agenda"

through drugs, sex and jazz saw them claim a place on the political agenda. In 1956, the co-founder of City Lights bookshop, Lawrence Ferlinghetti, published Allen Ginsberg's *Howl and Other Poems* and, as a result, landed himself in the back of a paddy wagon facing obscenity charges. He won the trial, which established a new legal standard for publishing contentious yet socially significant works.

Now, back to those dishonourably discharged servicemen and women.

Raise the bar

01 Vesuvio Café, North Beach
Loud bar favoured by the Beats.
02 Twin Peaks Tavern, The Castro
First known gay bar to ditch blacked-out windows.
03 Hippie Hill, Golden Gate Park
Alfresco drinking destination in The Summer of Love.

We can deduce that their influx into San Francisco, paired with the city's reputation for social activism, contributed to a growing LGBTQ community. Significant battles for equality were fought and eventually won here, with precursors such as the 1955 formation of the Daughters of Bilitis (the first national lesbian civil and political rights organisation) playing a significant role. The Daughters were also responsible for the first public gathering of lesbians in the US, which took place for a conference in 1960.

In 1966, what's thought to be the first LGBTQ-related riot in the US began with a disgruntled drag queen throwing a cup of coffee in the face of a prejudiced policeman. Known as the Compton's Cafeteria Riot, it propelled police brutality and discrimination towards transgender women and gay men onto the national agenda. And then, of course, there was charismatic city supervisor Harvey Milk. In 1977, he was one of the US's first openly gay men to be elected to office but tragically was assassinated alongside mayor George Moscone in 1978.

Bear with me as I rewind the clock slightly (there's a lot to cover in the 1960s and 1970s) to the founding of the Black Panther Party in Oakland in 1966. Huey P Newton and Bobby Seale established this national platform as a way to combat police brutality and oppression. The duo also saw value in grassroots action and established free health clinics and food programmes that provided breakfast to approximately 20,000 disadvantaged children a week. Despite forceful opposition from the FBI and criticism of the their sometimes violent approach, they played an integral role in the civil rights movement and inspired factions abroad in the UK, Australia, India and Algeria.

One year after the Black Panthers' founding, tie-dye-clad hippies inundated the grounds of the Golden Gate Park for the Human Be-In. This acid-fuelled festival was the precursor to the Summer of Love, which would influence pop culture from its Haight-Ashbury base. The hippie movement denounced capitalism, encouraged an anti-materialistic counterculture and boasted such supporters as Janis Joplin and Jimi Hendrix.

Often played down as a mere phase, the Summer of Love evolved into a powerful albeit subtle influencer and mobilised a radical generation of youths. This arguably catalysed the 1968 San Francisco State Strike (which, at five months, was the longest student strike in US history) and the 1969 to 1971 occupation of Alcatraz Island by the Indians of All Tribes and subsequently by the American Indian Red Power Movement. It also later sparked the 1977 Section 504 Sit-in, which demanded civil rights for the disabled. At 25 days, it became the longest ever occupation of a federal building in the US.

This round-up highlights a mere fraction of the city's prodigious number of organisations, people and events, all of which sparked progressive change. One thing, however, is plain: a revolutionary psyche has long been the Bay Area's prescribed zeitgeist. — (M)

i

ABOUT THE WRITER: Mikaela Aitken is the assistant editor for MONOCLE's books series. While in town, she lost a morning perusing the US history section at Green Apple Books and spent the rest of the day trying not to let her literary haul upset the balance on her bicycle.

ESSAY 08
Read all about it
The city's print media

———

Long before the city was pioneering digital products and technology, it was the hub for a vibrant community of writers and publishers.

*by Ed Stocker,
Monocle*

There's a commonly held perception on the US's West Coast that the country's best ideas start out there before migrating east and getting picked up by the rest of the country. The modern-day manifestation of this notion is the start-up acumen – and the gigabytes of software that it generates – that was born in and around San Francisco to be celebrated throughout the US and worldwide. Not bad for a place that can often feel more town than city, a Gold Rush boomer that sprung up at breakneck speed.

Indeed, the idea of San Francisco punching above its weight – given its relatively small population size – is a constant throughout its history. Yet stepping away from digital gizmos and Silicon Valley cash, one of the most important legacies of this success has been really rather analogue.

San Francisco has long had one of the most respected and diverse print-media landscapes in the US. The scene was born in the days of the adventurers and fortune-seekers who flooded into northern California and found themselves in need of a rag that covered their new home's scurrilous scandals. While many of those historic newspapers have long since folded, the *San Francisco Chronicle* – dating back to 1865 – still survives in what is by no means an easy print climate.

One of the most fascinating aspects of San Francisco's media scene has been the way in which it has realigned the country's traditional poles of influence. The long-held belief has been that any weighty magazine or internationally orientated newspaper needed to be based on the eastern seaboard; in other words, it needed to be near the nation's capital and facing Europe. The first to challenge that precept was arguably *Mother Jones*, a left-leaning non-profit founded in 1976, which showed you could be based in San Francisco and still bring out a current-affairs title. In many ways, argue its editors, it's a benefit to be publishing in San Francisco: if an event breaks late in the east or even in Europe,

the difference in time zones between the east and west coasts means that San Francisco is better positioned to react in a timely fashion.

Another standout is *Wired* (*see page 75*), which was founded in San Francisco in 1993 to cover the nexus of technology and society. When it was bought by media conglomerate Condé Nast it stubbornly refused to move – even though the majority of the other titles in the corporate stable are based in New York.

The most recent player on the scene is the excellent *California Sunday Magazine*. As its editor Doug McGray recently told me, the West Coast has plenty of cultural and commercial links with Asia and

"Stepping away from digital gizmos and Silicon Valley cash, one of the most important legacies of this success has been really rather analogue"

Latin America, so why not have a publication that covers stories from those regions? As the US's influence dips alongside that of Europe, and the international clout of China increases, there may be ever-greater reasons to have such a media outlet in San Francisco or other parts of the West Coast.

Of course, San Francisco has quite the literary tradition,

as the great fermenter of the
Beat Generation. Thanks to Jack
Kerouac et al, its freewheeling
counterculture ensured US writing
would never be the same. Ditto
gonzo luminary Hunter S
Thompson, who lived on the
California coast while writing his
tome on the Hell's Angels. Today
Dave Eggers – the original founder
of independent publisher (and
MONOCLE favourite) McSweeney's
– also calls the Bay Area home.

Maybe it has something to
do with the weather – that brisk
breeze and the fog that can
roll in from nowhere – but San
Franciscans are an introspective
bunch. While down south in Los
Angeles and San Diego they're far
too busy sunning themselves and
fretting about their bodies, San
Francisco has instead focused on
fomenting strong opinion and
scribbling it down. And it's a
pretty good read. — (M)

ABOUT THE WRITER: Ed Stocker is MONOCLE's
New York bureau chief and the editor of our US
travel guides, including yours truly.

ESSAY 09
Between The Rock and a hard place
Swimming from Alcatraz
———
San Francisco's island prison was believed to be inescapable – not least because of its treacherous waters. Today, many people are still putting that theory to the test.

by Bonnie Tsui, writer

I once took a night tour of Alcatraz. What I remember most was that the nearness of the island prison to downtown meant that inmates were often haunted by the sounds of life across the water. When city residents held New Year's Eve parties and noises of their revelry carried across the bay, the opposite shore would seem maddeningly close to the inmates. As a prison, The Rock was designed to break you into submission, and this was the ultimate torture: proximity.

Barely 2.5km offshore from San Francisco, Alcatraz was said to be escape-proof, the waters around it unswimmable. Nonetheless, in the nearly three decades that it was a functioning federal prison – it opened in 1934 and closed in 1963 – there were 14 escape attempts involving 36 prisoners. The most infamous and exhaustively planned attempt was that of Frank Morris and the Anglin brothers in June 1962. They tunnelled out of their cells using

"The water temperature (often about 12C or colder), vicious currents of six knots or faster, razor-sharp rocks and sharks were believed to make swimming impossible"

using computer modelling and historical tidal data shows a narrow window of opportunity in which they could have avoided being sucked out to sea, possibly emerging from the water in the headlands north of the Golden Gate Bridge. Debris from this landing would likely have washed up on Angel Island after the tide turned – and in fact this was where the FBI found a paddle and personal items linked to the men. Still, the most probable outcome for them was hypothermia and drowning.

One inmate, John Paul Scott, succeeded in swimming from the island to Fort Point on the southern end of the Golden Gate Bridge in December 1962. He and another prisoner had fashioned water wings from stolen rubber gloves and, while Scott's co-conspirator broke his ankle during the prison break and was recovered within minutes, Scott beached at Fort Point on an ebb tide. He was found unconscious, suffering from hypothermia, and after a stay at the Presidio hospital was soon brought back to Alcatraz.

Scott's was the only confirmed case of a prisoner reaching the shore by swimming. The water temperature (often about 12C or colder), vicious currents of six knots or faster, razor-sharp rocks and sharks were believed to make the task impossible. Scott proved it wasn't.

sharpened spoons, leaving their beds occupied by blankets and dummy heads constructed out of soap, loo roll and their own hair. By night, they entered the water in an inflated raft made from 50 stolen raincoats. The three men were never found but a recent study

Famous inmates

01 **Al Capone**
The most notorious gangster in US history.
02 **Robert Stroud**
Better known as the Birdman of Alcatraz.
03 **Roy Gardner**
Great US train robber and the most notorious escape artist of his time.

But swimmers on the outside had been testing the waters around Alcatraz since at least the 1920s. In 1933, the year before Alcatraz opened as a federal penitentiary, 17-year-old Anastasia Scott, whose father was stationed on the island, swam from Alcatraz to San Francisco in 43 minutes, accompanied by a rowboat. Two other San Francisco swimmers, Doris McLeod and Gloria Scigliano, made the swim shortly thereafter, to protest the decision to turn the island into a prison (McLeod did the two-way crossing in two hours). All three women – without wetsuits – were excellent swimmers with knowledge of the tide conditions; also critical to their success, of course, was that they were not required to escape by night or to subsist on a prison diet with little to no exercise.

In the years since these efforts, thousands of swimmers have made the journey, with the added benefit of tide charts, wetsuits and boat chaperones. Annual races and swimming events fill up months in advance, so many of us are compelled to test our own limits and the limits of the possible.

One autumn, I decided to swim from Alcatraz to San Francisco; it was a dare. A friend and I took up training in the waters around Aquatic Park, a sandy beach not far from Fort Point and the end point of most Alcatraz swims. From here you can venture into the Bay and get a feel for the strength of the currents, and the first time we swam there I experienced a queasy discomfort. It started with a tightness in my chest and a genuine anxiety of the kind that I hadn't felt for years when it came to swimming. My breath didn't come easily and I couldn't decide whether I should attribute that to the cold, which was crushing, or the wetsuit, which was unexpectedly confining. My friend smiled at me when we took a break to tread water and chat. "Relax," he said when he saw my face. "And breathe."

By the morning of our swim, I'd prepared myself for the cold and was familiar with the way in which the bay's currents on an outgoing tide could pull you with unnerving speed towards the open ocean. I knew that container ships could seem far away but come upon you in a matter of breaths. Our boat pilot, Gary Emich, was an open-water swimming legend who had just completed his 511th swim from Alcatraz to San Francisco (years later he would go on to break a world record with his 1,000th swim). I'd conditioned myself to follow my friend's advice: relax and breathe.

There were six of us swimming that day. The water temperature was 14C, the surface chopped with a light wind. We arrived at Alcatraz before 09.00 and jumped in on a flood tide. In photos from that morning, I am smiling. I look warmer than I feel, the sun glinting silver off my reflective goggles. The chilly water had a bite that managed to steal away my first breath and we regrouped for one last wave at our boat and its pilot. Then we turned for the city and swam. As I stroked through the water, I fell into a rhythm and pulled ahead. It was curious to turn to the side for a breath and be confronted with the full length of the Golden Gate Bridge with such Technicolor immediacy. It was like swimming in a postcard dream of San Francisco. — (M)

ABOUT THE WRITER: Bonnie Tsui is a frequent contributor to *The New York Times* and a member of the San Francisco Writers' Grotto. She's currently writing a book about swimming, which will be published by Algonquin Books.

ESSAY 10
Amazing greys
The fog
———

It comes out of nowhere, descending rapidly to chill and isolate. But the fog in San Francisco is more inspiring than inconvenient and viewed as a beloved part of the city's fabric.

by Tomos Lewis, Monocle

The engine of our little fishing boat whirs to life off Fisherman's Wharf on a warm, clear day in early summer. A few boats along, two huge glossy grey seals are rolling in the water, flanking a fishing craft that has just returned from the bay; the fishermen on board are picking through their catch and the seals have caught wind of it, yelping for a piece of the action.

We chug out of the wharf and the captain accelerates into the open water, where we cheer and yelp as the boat slams into the aggressive chop on its route west to the Golden Gate Bridge. The greenery of the Presidio and the grand silhouette of the Palace of Fine Arts (*see page 107*) slip by in the distance to our left. Tiny figures on the beach, some basking in the sun, some with kites that dot the blue sky with specks of colour, are visible through the spray as we head on over the water.

All of a sudden, out of nowhere, the crisp blue day disappears and we're engulfed by one of San Francisco's most notable natural attributes: the fog. It has, as is its way, snuck up on us without warning, snatching away the scenery and leaving us stranded in a sightless netherworld.

It's dark and grey – like a heavy, old duvet shrouding us from the world and the waters beyond. The boat slows and drifts forward through the waves. The captain's microphone crackles to life above the eerie lapping of the water, cutting through the strange quiet that the descending fog has brought with it. "There she is," the captain says. "Look up and to your left."

We do, and looming out of the fog-induced gloaming is the Golden Gate Bridge, imposing and grand and only partially visible in the slow-moving swirl of grey around it. In the fog, from below, it looks like the gateway to a world in a Tolkien novel.

Warm air from the land mingling with cold air from the sea is a feature of the climate all along the California coast but in San Francisco the resulting fog has woven itself into the city's life, culture and folklore. These days it even has a name: Karl (after a character in the 2003 Tim Burton film *Big Fish*) and an online persona (Karl likes to update San Franciscans on the weather and provide clothing advice when he's due to pay a visit).

For many, there's undoubtedly a romance that the fog has evoked over

"Warm air from the land mingling with cold air from the sea is a climate feature all along the California coast but in San Francisco the resulting fog has woven itself into the city's life, culture and folklore"

the years, elevating the everyday into something special. In few other sports stadiums, for example, do tendrils of fog slide like a veil across the upper tiers of the arena and down into the bowl of the stadium below, as they do at AT&T Park, the home of the San Francisco Giants major league baseball team.

The fog varies depending on the time of year and which part of the city you're in. There are two types that are most common in San Francisco: advection and tule. The former, which arrives in the summer, is pale and wispy, like the phenomenon the poet Carl Sandburg once described: "The fog comes on little cat feet. It sits looking over harbor and city on silent haunches and then moves on." The latter type is dark, brooding and grey, like the kind that has enveloped our fishing boat. "When the city is all covered with fog, it's like living inside a great grey pearl," wrote celebrated *San Francisco Chronicle* columnist Herb Caen of the city's convection fog.

In literature and music, too, the fog is often a bit player in the unfolding narrative, playing cameo roles that conjure either the isolation or the communal spirit that can result from being enveloped within it. Jack Kerouac famously wrote about it in *On the Road*. Upon leaving the confines of the city, "It seemed like a matter of minutes when we began rolling in the foothills before Oakland and suddenly reached a height and saw stretched out ahead of us the fabulous white city of San Francisco on her eleven mystic hills with the blue Pacific and its advancing wall of potato-patch fog

Explore the water

01 Captain Kirk's San Francisco Sailing
Either partake in the sailing or sit back and enjoy the view.
02 City Kayak
Waterfront tours for first-time and experienced paddlers.
03 Red and White Fleet
Hop on board San Francisco's original bay cruise.

beyond, and smoke and goldenness in the late afternoon of time."

The advancing wall of fog that Kerouac describes continues to inspire writers. In *Hollyhocks in the Fog: Selected San Francisco Poems*, August Kleinzahler explores the intertwining of nature and the human experience in his adopted city. He likens the notion of the natural fog to the haze created by the technology sectors that have transformed the city over the past three decades, and their impact on the hordes of Silicon Valley commuters who work within them.

If there's an isolating quality to the fog – whether natural or manmade – in Kleinzahler's work, Ingram Marshall chooses to recognise another facet of it. A contemporary classical composer based in the Bay Area, he has long used the fog and the dampening of the atmosphere that it brings with it as a source of inspiration. His notable set of "Fog Tropes" compositions play with the sounds of foghorns in the mist, at once lonely and a source of reassurance.

As the waves beneath the Golden Gate Bridge rock our little fishing boat in the fog, the captain revs up the engine once again and we begin heading back to land. But as we turn, a lone figure emerges through the veil of the mist: a kite-surfer, carving alone through the waves, dragged by the breeze out of the grey and towards the sunlight on the other side of the bridge. The fog in San Francisco, it seems, is never one's captor for long. — (M)

ABOUT THE WRITER: Tomos Lewis is MONOCLE's Toronto bureau chief. You'll be glad to know that he and his fellow voyagers made it out of Karl's clutches in one piece.

ESSAY 11

City of innovation
The soul of San Francisco

With its progressive attitudes and entrepreneurial sense of adventure, San Francisco has become a place where beliefs drive change.

by Nancy Pelosi, Democratic leader of the House of Representatives

San Francisco's namesake is Saint Francis of Assisi. He's our patron saint and his song is our anthem: "Lord, make me an instrument of your peace. Where there is hatred, let me sow love. Where there is darkness, let me sow light." I'm very proud of these values.

Indeed, the wonderful thing about San Francisco is that people act upon their beliefs. Whether it's protecting or expanding individual rights, preserving the environment, or the fight for jobs, justice and peace, everybody knows their purpose and has a plan.

Our city has a rich history of leadership. We're the city of the Golden Gate, the city where the UN charter was signed, the city that led the way for LGBTQ rights and faced down the darkest days of HIV/Aids.

During the height of the HIV epidemic many people moved to San Francisco – either because they weren't well received at home or because they were simply better received here. The mobilisation to raise awareness about Aids – which started out west – benefited our country by advancing acceptance and, in many ways, making the US more American. I truly believe that the activism surrounding HIV/Aids accelerated the forward movement of LGBTQ equality issues, from the first domestic partnerships and full marriage equality to comprehensive hate-crimes legislation and ending "Don't ask, don't tell" and many other issues.

"We're blessed with other beautiful diversity: Asian-Pacific Americans, Hispanic and African-Americans. In San Francisco, the beauty is in the mix"

While I grew up in Baltimore, my husband was born and raised in San Francisco. It was comfortable for me to move here, as a progressive Democrat. This is a capital of innovation, forward-thinking and entrepreneurial in both its infrastructure and ideas. That's represented in the innovative private-public partnerships that have sustained our city's treasured recreation areas such as the Presidio, at no cost to the taxpayer. It's also shown in San Francisco's leadership in the technology sector and the progressive spirit of activism that suffuses our community.

The other thing I love about San Francisco is that it's a very Italian-American city. We always say here that everybody is Italian or wants to be Italian. Of course, a lot of the Italians have moved out and today we're blessed with other beautiful diversity: Asian-Pacific Americans, Hispanic and African-Americans. In San Francisco, the beauty is in the mix.

I feel sad for my colleagues who have such plain districts. No honour is greater for me than that of representing the people of the beautiful city of San Francisco. — (M)

San Francisco politicians
—
01 **Willie Brown**
A former mayor who had a cameo in *The Godfather Part III*.
02 **Dianne Feinstein**
The city's first female mayor reintroduced cable cars.
03 **Harvey Milk**
California's first openly gay elected official.

ⓘ

ABOUT THE WRITER: Nancy Pelosi is the Democratic leader of the House of Representatives and has represented San Francisco for 30 years.

ESSAY 12

Old and new
Ode to Oakland

It may have a gritty reputation but this city across the bay is witnessing winds of change. One resident reports.

by Elena Ruiz, writer

Oakland pride has always lived in my bloodstream as a reminder of the place that raised me. This city – just across the bay from San Francisco and yet so distinct – makes room for it all. Hills, flatlands, ports and the inner city fuse to create diverse groups of people that help make the place unique. But then again, I'm bound to say that: I was born and brought up in the city, living in six different neighbourhoods during the course of 14 years.

It's true that Oakland might not have the best reputation, long dogged by horror headlines of its homicide rates. But that's just one side of the story. The other is one of vibrancy and change – and

difficult times for some, as new arrivals have pushed up property prices, causing a number of working and middle-class long-term residents to abandon their hometown altogether. In some senses, it's been part of a cycle as those pushed out of San Francisco due to spiralling costs have looked further afield to relatively cheaper property stock across the bay.

Downtown Oakland, with its increasing number of coffee shops and craft-beer bars, is arguably the place that most feels the winds of gentrification in the city. And yet, conversely, it's these changes that have also made Oakland cling to its traditions. The city has pushed its arts scene in a bid to maintain its cultural identity.

Indeed, every first Friday of the month, Telegraph Avenue – a long thoroughfare that runs from downtown to Berkeley – plays host to part of the Art Murmur programme. Everyone is welcome and the minimally lit throng of people sway to music emanating from a host of different stages. Art galleries open their doors to the public for free, while retailers hawk their wares, from plants and paintings to clothing and jewellery (and pretty much

"Oakland has an undefeatable energy and it's important to remember the people that cultivated that liveliness"

> **Oakland highlights**
> —
> 01 **Grand Lake Theater**
> A historical art deco cinema
> in Lake Merritt.
> 02 **Shan Dong Restaurant**
> A no-frills institution with
> hand-pulled noodles.
> 03 **Oakland Museum of
> California**
> Excellent exhibitions in a
> brutalist building.

everything else in between). It was during these parties growing up that I was first able to test my independence – while absorbing some of the richest cultural life that the bay has to offer.

Further down on Telegraph Avenue – and its parallel street, Broadway – are reminders of what makes this city so culturally rich and aesthetically pleasing. The Fox and Paramount theatres are two prime examples. The latter (*see page 137*) is a breathtaking building from 1931: one of the finest examples of art deco in the country and a national historic landmark. The Fox Theatre – also doubling as Oakland School for the Arts – has long provided Oakland juniors and high school attendees (myself included) the opportunity to hone passions in the heart of the city centre.

If ever proof were needed that Oakland's diversity is alive and well, it's through the food. Downtown Oakland counteracts gentrification by authentically representing the diversity that exists there. Chinatown has long been the place I take visitors for cheap dim sum, *banh mi* and boba tea. Indian, Mexican, US, Jamaican, African and Japanese restaurants line the surrounding streets.

Oakland has an undefeatable energy and it's important to remember the people that cultivated that liveliness; it will persistently strive to accommodate new residents while tending to the old ones. It's the newcomers' responsibility to educate themselves about the past and present – and make sure that they treat the city with the respect it deserves. Oakland is a place to indulge one's senses, as long as that means staying inquisitive. I thank those who instilled these values in me as I grew up and hope to pass them onto the next generation here – whether that's a new resident, an old-timer or simply a visitor hopping over from across the bay. — (M)

ABOUT THE WRITER: Elena Ruiz is an essayist and journalist who recently published *Locus: The Trajectory of Gentrification in Oakland.*

Culture
—— Colourful canvas

Tony Bennett crooned about leaving his heart in San Francisco in 1962 and it's a sentiment that continues to chime with many artists today – from painters to poets, songwriters to theatre producers, and the gamut of creative industries in between. Despite concerns that soaring living costs are pricing such artists out of the city, San Francisco remains one of the most vibrant cultural centres in the country.

The city boasts one of the nation's oldest ballet companies and its comedy and theatre pedigrees are among the finest in the US. Its history of activism has also long blended with the arts, from the birth of the hippie movement and the rise of the Beat authors to the advent of protest-theatre and the creation of the rainbow flag.

All this – plus a robust roster of commercial galleries, independent museums and live-music venues – ensures that San Francisco continues to be a muse for artists and visitors alike.

Cinemas
Screen stars

①
The Castro Theatre, The Castro
On with the show

Named after the street and neighbourhood that it occupies, the ornate Castro Theatre has been around for almost a century. Built in 1922 by theatre entrepreneurs the Nasser brothers, it now shows mostly independent flicks in its cavernous 1,400-seat auditorium.

Located in one of the US's first gay neighbourhoods, the Castro celebrates diverse films and hosts the vibrant San Francisco International LGBTQ Film Festival. It also features regular sing-along showings: we suspect you'll either love or hate them.
429 Castro Street, 94114
+1 415 621 6120
castrotheatre.com

San Francisco on film

01 The Maltese Falcon, 1941: One of the greatest films of Hollywood's golden age features Humphrey Bogart as the screen's quintessential private detective opposite Mary Astor. An iconic and defining film noir.

02 Vertigo, 1958: Alfred Hitchcock's masterpiece was voted the best film ever in a poll of critics by the British Film Institute in 2012. The complex tale of obsession features James Stewart and Kim Novak.

03 Milk, 2008: Sean Penn's performance as Harvey Milk, the first openly gay person elected to public office in California, won the Academy Award for best actor. The film recalls a defining episode in the city's history.

04 Blue Jasmine, 2013: Cate Blanchett won the Academy Award for best actress for her role in this superb drama by writer and director Woody Allen.

2

Clay Theatre, Pacific Heights
Down to earth

This classic single-screen theatre was opened by media tycoons Robert and Marshall Naify in 1910 and has been an integral part of San Francisco's Pacific Heights neighbourhood ever since. The neon sign hanging from the squat building hints at its heritage.

Today, the art deco structure features plush, modern seating and a hi-tech sound system. Come to catch anything from a US cult classic to a foreign film.
2261 Fillmore Street, 94115
+1 415 561 9921
landmarktheatres.com/san-francisco/clay-theatre

Dude looks like a lady

3

Roxie Theater, Mission District
Think pink

In business since 1909, the Roxie Theater – with its iconic pink signage – has been a landmark of the Mission for more than a century. But this cinema offers more than films: it invites filmmakers, entertainers and educators to engage with the audience and discuss the films they're watching.

The Roxie screens independent, arthouse and documentary films in the 234-seat Big Roxie, the world's second-oldest continually operating cinema, as well as a smaller 49-seat space.
3117 16th Street, 94103
+1 415 863 1087
roxie.com

Theatre and dance companies
Setting the stage

Home-grown talent

01 American Conservatory Theater: The non-profit ACT was founded in 1965 and today produces major shows at both The Strand and The Geary Theater. It also has a training school dedicated to bringing on emerging actors.
act-sf.org

02 San Francisco Ballet: With a history that stretches back to 1933, the San Francisco Ballet is one of the best-respected outfits in the US. Its repertoire runs from classical through to contemporary.
sfballet.org

03 Magic Theatre: Spotlighting plucky new plays and writers, Magic Theatre has been welcoming artists for more than 50 years. Many of its plays have moved onto stages around the world.
magictheatre.org

①
Cheaper Than Therapy, Union Square
House of fun

Comedy club Cheaper Than Therapy offers stand-up evenings at the Shelton Theater in downtown San Francisco every Thursday, Friday, Saturday and Sunday.

The club's producers – Scott Simpson, Eloisa Bravo and Jon Allen – are longstanding comedians in their own right and appear on stage alongside guest acts. The weekly ritual of some comedy and post-show beers at Chelsea Place, a bar around the corner, is a must for mature audiences (21 years and above).
533 Sutter Street, 94102
+1 512 586 4401
cttcomedy.com

Live venues
Sounds of the city

①
Audium, Japantown
Now hear this
In 1967, trumpeter and composer Stanley Shaff, along with audio engineer Douglas MacEachern, created what they called the only "audio-art theatre space" in the world. It's fitted with 176 speakers, each of which plays a different role in every "performance".

The 49 audience members sit in the round and are encouraged to close their eyes as Shaff's compositions flow around them.
1616 Bush Street, 94109
+1 415 771 1616
audium.org

2
Curran, Tenderloin
Staying Curran(t)

This beaux arts theatre, named after the producer Homer Curran, opened its doors in 1922 and has since hosted more than 8,000 performances. Following extensive renovations – which saw each and every crystal of its prized 1.5 tonne chandelier removed and polished – it returned to the city's arts scene with the coming-of-age musical *Fun Home* in 2017.

The 1,600-seat Curran offers a capacious and beautiful setting in which to take in the vanguard of US theatre. Plus the elegant marble bar in the airy lobby keeps things interesting in the intermission – not least because it's supposedly haunted by the spirit of Hewlett Tarr, who was killed by armed thieves while working in the box office in 1933.

445 Geary Street, 94102
+1 415 358 1220
sfcurran.com

Live music

01 The Masonic, Nob Hill:
Opened in 1958, this
mid-century modern
building (*see page 111*)
sits atop Nob Hill. Built as
the HQ for a Californian
Masonic organisation, the
3,300-seat venue became
a full-time music venue in
1995 and was renovated
in 2014. The intimate
two-tiered space has
hosted acts such as Sting
and Trombone Shorty.
sfmasonic.com

**02 SFJazz Center, Hayes
Valley:** Built in 2013, the
SFJazz Center has quickly
become the crown jewel
in the city's vibrant jazz
scene. The building's sleek
exterior matches the
bright, state-of-the-art,
700-seat auditorium
space, which attracts the
likes of Gregory Porter
and Dee Dee Bridgewater
alongside the country's
best jazz musicians. "San
Francisco is the perfect
city for a project like this
because it's a city that
celebrates newness,
exploration and creativity,"
says SFJazz founder
Randall Kline.
sfjazz.org

**03 The Chapel, Mission
District:** You'll find The
Chapel in a 1914 building
with arched ceilings that
measure more than 12
metres in height. Since
founding the venue in
2012, Jack Knowles has
ensured that it's about
more than just music: if
you're feeling peckish,
head to The Vestry
restaurant, and when you
fancy a drink make a
beeline for the Chapel Bar.
thechapelsf.com

Museums
On and off the wall

①
SFMoma, Soma
Top fog

Founded in 1935, SFMoma was
originally housed in the War
Memorial Veterans Building in
the Fillmore District. In the 1990s
it moved to this Mario Botta-
designed building, which reopened
in 2016 with an expansion –
inspired by the water and fog of
San Francisco Bay – by Snøhetta.
   The impressive public space is
filled with light and art and plays
host to performance, photography
and architecture exhibitions.
Visitors are greeted by the artworks
of Richard Serra, Sol LeWitt and
Amy Ellingson.
151 Third Street, 94103
+1 415 357 4000
sfmoma.org

❷
Contemporary Jewish Museum, Soma
Back to the future

Far from a history museum, this forward-thinking establishment – as its name implies – explores Jewish identity and culture. Founded in 1984 in a former power station, and with a striking steel extension designed by Daniel Libeskind in 2008 (*see page 113*), the CJM has hosted many Jewish artists (including *The New Yorker* cartoonist Roz Chast), curators and public figures.

There's also a Wise Sons (*see page 35*) outpost that offers tasty salads, sandwiches and bagels.
736 Mission Street, 94103
+1 415 655 7800
thecjm.org

Three more museums

01 Legion of Honor, Sea Cliff: One of the city's most beautiful museum complexes, the Legion of Honor has a collection that spans four millennia. The French neoclassical building sits atop Lincoln Park, with stunning views of San Francisco Bay and the Pacific. Tickets include same-day admission for the De Young Museum (*see opposite*).
legionofhonor.famsf.org

02 Yerba Buena Center for the Arts, Soma: Since the 1990s, the YBCA has supported and celebrated a range of performance, visual and film artists from the Bay Area and beyond. Shows are spread across two landmark buildings and, true to its mission of inclusivity in the arts, the centre offers pay-what-you-can membership.
ybca.org

03 Moad, South Beach: The small but excellent Museum of the African Diaspora opened in 2005 and exhibits the work of artists who explore the experience of African diasporas throughout history, from slavery in the US to the present day.
moadsf.org

The Beat goes on

In the 1950s the authorities saw the Beat generation's words as tawdry: too absorbed in free thought, sex, drugs and jaunty jazz. Today these works – such as Jack Kerouac's *On The Road* – are US classics. Visit The Beat Museum in North Beach for a full round-up.
kerouac.com

4
Tenderloin Museum, Tenderloin
Neighbourhood watch

Dedicated to the Tenderloin, this museum offers a history of its inhabitants. Through walking tours, interactive exhibition spaces and public programmes, visitors learn about the notorious neighbourhood at the beating heart of the city.

Drop by to discover the stories and struggles of individual immigrants and hear about the Tenderloin's speakeasies, recording studios and history-making gay rights activism.
398 Eddy Street, 94102
+1 415 351 1912
tenderloinmuseum.org

3
De Young Museum, Golden Gate Park
Park life

Founded in 1895, this fine-arts museum reopened in 2005 with a dramatic new facility that fully integrates with the natural landscape (*see page 114*).

The permanent collection is wonderfully diverse – with woodcarvings, paintings, black-and-white photographs and textiles – and the colourful temporary exhibitions feature everything from fashion to featherwork. Plus in summer it opens late for live music, screenings and more.
50 Hagiwara Tea Garden Drive, 94118
+1 415 750 3600
deyoung.famsf.org

⑤
Musée Mécanique, Fisherman's
Wharf
Child's play

Founded by the late Edward
Galland Zelinsky, Musée
Mécanique is more of an arcade
than a museum: don't go expecting
white walls and glass display cases.
Zelinsky spent his entire life
collecting antique arcade games
and musical instruments and
today this colourful and chaotic
venue holds one of the world's
largest collections of coin-operated
machines, all of which are kept
in their original condition – hand
cranks and all. Not for everyone
but there's certainly no place like it.
*Pier 45, Fisherman's Wharf, 94133
+1 415 346 2000
museemecaniquesf.com*

All that jazz

**01 Boom Boom Room,
Fillmore District:** A
funky club where dancing
to jazz, blues, boogie,
groove and soul music is
encouraged. The sultry
juke joint plays live music
six nights a week.
boomboomroom.com
**02 Mr Tipple's Recording
Studio, Civic Center:**
This tucked-away
recording studio doubles
as a bar, combining the
owner's passion for live
music and zingy cocktails.
mrtipplessf.com
**03 Club Deluxe, Haight-
Ashbury:** Evocative of
New York's jazz houses,
the glowing red lights,
sound of brass and
Giovanni's Pizza are all
the rage on Haight Street.
clubdeluxe.co
04 Bix, Jackson Square:
At this supper club and
saloon down an alley in
Jackson Square, live jazz
sets the scene while
uniformed bartenders
serve some of the best
cocktails in town.
bixrestaurant.com

Art and age

The quirky Maritime Museum
in Fisherman's Wharf is housed
in one of San Francisco's finest
art deco buildings, which is
adorned with whimsical murals
by Sargent Johnson and Hilaire
Hiler and also accommodates a
care home for the elderly.
+1 415 561 7100

Public galleries and exhibition venues
Art for all

das Plakat

①
Letterform Archive, Potrero Hill
Prints charming

Based in a bright and airy
loft space in the residential
neighbourhood of Potrero Hill,
this nonprofit trove of floor-to-
ceiling shelves is stacked with
fonts and letterforms. Graphic
designer Rob Saunders collected
letter arts for 40 years and founded
the archive in 2015 to share his
personal collection with the public.

The vibrant compilation
covers 2,000 years of calligraphy,
graphic design and typography
in its 40,000 works. Visits are
by appointment.
*1001 Mariposa Street 307, 94107
+1 415 802 7485
letterformarchive.org*

All together now
—
The Fort Mason Center served
as a US Army facility for more
than a century. When it was
decommissioned in the 1970s,
it was transformed into a
cultural hub, providing a home
for theatre companies, music
schools and more.
fortmason.org

Commercial galleries
Wonder walls

③
Pier 24, South Beach
Behind the lens

Pier 24 occupies a 2,600 sq m
converted warehouse that stretches
out directly beneath the Bay Bridge
from the Embarcadero. Opened
in 2010 by the Pilara Foundation,
the space showcases photography,
from contemporary Bay Area
snaps to historical images of
San Francisco and early US
colour photographs.
    It's now home to the permanent
collection of the foundation and
hosts a series of rotating exhibitions
by influential US photographers
such as Lee Friedlander. Entry is
free but by appointment only.
Pier 24, 94105
+1 415 512 7424
pier24.org

②
Minnesota Street Project, Dogpatch
Making spaces

This string of three warehouses
was opened in 2016 by art
collectors Deborah and Andy
Rappaport, who aimed to plug a
gap in the city's artistic offering:
affordable studio and gallery
space. Now, with about a dozen
(mostly commercial) galleries and
more than 35 artists' studios, the
range of contemporary art is both
impressive and accessible.
    The main building (once a prop
warehouse where the Grateful Dead
built their sets) was redesigned by
Jensen Architects and now has a
restaurant by chef Daniel Patterson.
1275 Minnesota Street, 94107
+1 415 243 0825
minnesotastreetproject.com

①
Fraenkel Gallery, Financial District
Best shot

With a focus on photography
and its relationship with other
artistic fields, Fraenkel Gallery
hosts exhibitions that revisit the
medium's history right up to
the present day.
    Since its opening in 1979,
the gallery has represented a
range of artists: Walker Evans, Sol
LeWitt and Hiroshi Sugimoto, to
name a few. Its sister programme,
FraenkelLab, opened in Civic
Center in 2016 to display art of
any medium.
4th Floor, 49 Geary Street, 94108
+1 415 981 2661
fraenkelgallery.com

Over the rainbow

The rainbow flag – the symbol
of gay rights movements
worldwide, iterations of which
have graced the façades
of buildings from the White
House to London's Palace of
Westminster – was created in
San Francisco in 1978 by the
late artist Gilbert Baker.
gilbertbaker.com

③
Berggruen Gallery, South Beach
Near and far

A member of the Art Dealers Association of America, the Berggruen Gallery has a roster that extends from the Bay Area figurative works to US postwar artists and emerging contemporary talent from around the world.

Established in 1970, it specialises in contemporary art and 20th-century US and European works. Originally located at Grant Avenue, the current Hawthorne address – next door to the city's Gagosian Gallery – is a hotspot for the Californian art scene.
10 Hawthorne Street, 94105
+1 415 781 4629
berggruen.com

❷
Adrian Rosenfeld Gallery, Dogpatch
Art and aperitifs

Adrian Rosenfeld's (*pictured*) eponymous gallery is located in one of Minnesota Street Project's (*see opposite*) three warehouses.

The contemporary-art gallery, designed by US architect Thomas Ryan, collaborates with international art dealers to present four exhibitions each year. There's also a library with tomes on various collectors and collections, and a well-stocked bar – should you need help loosening your purse strings.
1150 25th Street, 94107
+1 415 285 2841

⑤
Anthony Meier Fine Arts,
Pacific Heights
Neighbourhood gallery

The home of Anthony Meier Fine
Arts is as striking as the collections
within. The four-storey gothic
revival house was built in 1911 and
is a landmark in the Pacific Heights
neighbourhood. "We like to think
that we're unlike any other gallery
in the city," says owner Anthony
Meier, who opened his exhibition
space in 1996.
    The gallery hosts five shows a
year, dedicated to both emerging
and mid-career artists such as
sculptor Leonardo Drew and
painter Sarah Cain.
1969 California Street, 94109
+1 415 351 1400
anthonymeierfinearts.com

④
Jessica Silverman Gallery,
Tenderloin
Expect the unexpected

This contemporary gallery,
founded in 2008, supports artists
no matter their age or experience.
"Our youngest artist is 26 and the
oldest is in their 70s," says owner
Jessica Silverman (*pictured*).
    Embracing all artistic media,
the gallery presents its artists to a
global audience, selling works to
renowned museums such as New
York's Moma and London's Tate.
As if that isn't enough, Silverman
is also the curator of Fused Space,
an exhibition studio associated with
designer Yves Béhar.
488 Ellis Street, 94102
+1 415 255 9508
jessicasilvermangallery.com

Media round-up
Eyes and ears

① Media
Text and the city

The go-to daily newspaper here is the broadsheet ❶ *San Francisco Chronicle*, which was established in 1865 and has been garlanded with six Pulitzer Prizes.

When it comes to magazines, ❷ *Mother Jones* first hit newsstands in 1976 as a bimonthly targeted at politically progressive readers; now it's a rare example of a magazine that has balanced the digital realm with a loyal following for its printed pages. For stories on life across the Golden State, ❸ *The California Sunday Magazine* – first published in 2014 as an insert in the Sunday editions of national newspapers before being turned into a bimonthly in its own right – features long-form reports on subjects from crime to agriculture.

Finally, architecture and design enthusiasts should pick up ❹ *Dwell*, published six times a year, and skateboarding and music fans should look no further than ❺ *Thrasher*, first published in 1981.

② Kiosks
Get your reads here

With the help of design studios, San Francisco has taken the initiative to transform its cylindrical news kiosks into cultural and entrepreneurial outposts.

An extension of the popular Heath Ceramics (*see page 53*), the shelves at Heath Newsstand are stocked with publications from near and far, hard-to-find prints and the local daily paper.

A reflection of the city's diversity, Fog City News carries the largest variety of magazines in the Bay Area, with more than 700 foreign publications alone. And, while you're there, take a moment to sample one of the hundreds of imported premium chocolates – it would be rude not to.
2900 18th Street, 94110
+1 415 873 9209
heathceramics.com;
455 Market Street #125, 94105
+1 415 543 7400
fogcitynews.com

Radio and podcasts

01 **KQED (88.5MHz):** Northern California's public station carries national NPR programmes as well as city-made shows. The most popular is *Bay Curious*, a broadcast and podcast on the Bay Area's underexplored corners.
kqed.org

02 **The Commonwealth Club of California:** The longest-running weekly radio broadcast in the US – first aired in 1924 – hosts discussions on topics such as politics and astronomy.
commonwealthclub.org/podcasts

03 **San Francisco History Podcast:** An archive of audio explorations of various chapters from the city's history, including Mark Twain's response to the 1906 earthquake.
sparkletack.com

04 **The Intersection:** Unpicking the untold stories of neighbourhoods from Haight Ashbury to Tenderloin. Produced with local radio station KALW.
theintersection.fm

05 **99% Invisible:** Produced in Oakland, 99% Invisible traces the design history of everyday objects such as the fortune cookie.
99percentinvisible.org

Simply fascinating…

Design and architecture
── Building the city's identity

The founding fathers of San Francisco recognised beauty when they saw it, picking a site with undulating hills and epic Pacific Ocean views for what was initially a tiny settlement. Fast-forward to today and looks still play a huge part in the city's make-up. You could spend days wandering the neighbourhoods, marvelling at the intricate Victorian frontages.

Hidden beneath the city's good looks, however, is the potential threat posed by the San Andreas Fault: in 1906 much of the city was destroyed by a quake. The result? Today, an eclectic mix of art deco, modernist and shiny contemporary structures define the skyline.

San Francisco's architecture isn't just a reflection of the city's topography but also a realisation of its mighty aspirations, from Gold Rush mecca to technology incubator. Packed into its small space are plenty of edifices – and symbolic crowd-pleasers – to rival any of the world's great metropolises.

Bridges
Spectacular spans

① Richmond-San Rafael Bridge
Size matters

From afar, this elegant 1956 bridge looks more like a rollercoaster, thanks to the way in which the sea-level section springs up and grows legs.

What's most impressive about the cantilever and continuous truss bridge is the sheer scale of it: about 9km in length (some have questioned why it needed to be built in such a wide gap between the two stretches of land). And innocuous as the site looks, it sits in a seismic hotbed, just a few kilometres from the Hayward Fault and slightly further from the San Andreas Fault. Take a mini road trip (via the Muir Woods, perhaps) to see it and then cross it into the Eastern Bay.

② Oakland Bay Bridge
Huge undertaking

This was the longest steel structure in the world when it was completed in 1936 and placing the original 55 steel tubes in the middle of the bay was a massive feat of engineering.

The western part of the bridge, from the city to Yerba Buena Island (two suspension bridges divided by a central anchorage), was given a seismic retrofit in 2004. The eastern part was overhauled in 2013 with a dual-lane, single-towered suspension bridge over the high, shipping-lane section, which turns into a skyway structure as it drops lower.

The west of the bridge was lit up with 25,000 LEDs to mark its 75th anniversary, a move so popular it was made permanent in 2016.

Catch you on the flip side!

③

Golden Gate Bridge
Symbol of a city

The defining image of San
Francisco, the Golden Gate Bridge
was named after the entrance to
San Francisco Bay from the Pacific.
Opened in 1937 after four years
of construction (during which 11
workers died), it was the world's
longest suspension bridge for
just under 30 years (it now barely
makes the top 15).

The colour it's painted is
known as "international orange"
and was chosen by consultant
architect Irving Morrow to be
consistent with the warm colours
of the surrounding landmasses and
contrast with the cool tones of the
sky and sea. Hard to argue that he
didn't make a fine choice.

Reel fact

The setting
of a thrilling
James Bond
fight scene

Victorian
Pre-quake classics

Victorian style

It's no surprise that San
Francisco has so many
Victorian houses (some
50,000) given its Gold Rush
past. The city boomed during
the early years of Victorian
architecture: it went from having
a few hundred residents in the
1840s to tens of thousands a
few years later. These Victorian
homes and their varying levels
of ornamentation reflect the
shift during this period.

Victorian homes here can
be divided into three categories,
the first of which is Italianate.
These date from the 1840s
to the 1880s and are simple
timber structures with flat
frontages and roofs; many burnt
down after the 1906 quake.

Next are the more stylised
"stick" homes, sometimes
referred to as Eastlakes, which
feature wood from surrounding
redwood forests in the form of
overlaid sticks on façades in
geometric patterns.

The final category is Queen
Anne, with big porches, turrets
and more elaborate façades. It's
these colourful houses, often
dripping with floral motifs, that
were popularised as "painted
ladies" from the late 1970s.

As for where to see all
of the above? Alamo Square
is a good starting point. As are
the Mission, Lower Haight and
Haight-Ashbury.

❶
500 Capp Street, Mission District
Experimental abode

Part arts project, part architectural exploration, this 1886 Italianate-style home was the residence of eccentric conceptual artist David Ireland from the 1970s until a few years before his death in 2009. It was refurbished by Jensen Architects and opened to the public in 2016.

Ireland turned the house into a living experiment, doing things such as attaching rocks (he called them his "turds") to the ceiling. The curved wall upstairs is unusual for Italianate houses in the city.
500 Capp Street, 94110
+1 415 872 9240
500cappstreet.org

②
The Haas-Lilienthal House, Pacific Heights
Time capsule

Named after the Haas and Lilienthal families, who lived here from its construction in 1886 until 1972, this home is a great example of Queen Anne architecture.

The interiors are largely untouched and original furnishings provide insight into 20th-century upper-middle-class life; don't miss the original fireplace in the dining room and the stained glass in the two bedrooms upstairs. There's also a crack in the wall just off the grand staircase from the 1906 earthquake – left as a sign of good fortune.
2007 Franklin Street, 94109
+1 415 441 3000
sfheritage.org/haas-lilienthal-house

Presidio
Repurposed military base

①
Fort Winfield Scott, Presidio
Shore line of defence

Fort Winfield Scott was once in charge of the city's coastal defence and housed 17 batteries – mounted gun stations that were constructed and manned between 1891 and 1946 – and army barracks.

Its design embraces the mission revival style, closely linked to the southwest's Spanish heritage. The early 20th-century buildings have flat stucco façades, curved silhouetted shapes that mimic mission architecture and tiled gable roofs. The World Economic Forum opened its Center for the Fourth Industrial Revolution in one of the buildings in early 2017.
Ralston Avenue, 94129

②
Officers' Club, Presidio
Top-ranking heritage site

Of the Presidio's 800 buildings, 470 are historic landmarks. But none have the same heritage as the Officers' Club, which retains its original adobe walls from 1776.

Bypass the dining room – remodelled in the 1930s – and head to the Mesa room, where the walls have been stripped to reveal the building's various guises: mission revival, Victorian-style red-brick and wooden-slatted fireplace, and the original adobe. Oh, and the building has a rather good Mexican restaurant called Arguello, if you're feeling peckish.
50 Moraga Avenue, 94129
+ 1 415 561 4400
presidio.gov

Park life

Check out San Francisco's famous parking spot-sized "parklets" (*see page 70*), which can be found all over town. These small spaces are highly sought after by emerging designers and architects, who are raring to show the city what they're capable of.

③
Officers' Row, Presidio
Historic housing

Down the road from the Inn at the Presidio (*see page 18*), Officers' Row is the only Civil War street in San Francisco. Today the houses are used by schools and small businesses but they were originally built for officers and their families. In the 1880s they were beautified with picket fences, street lamps and flower-filled gardens.

Building 2, built in 1862, is of particular interest, used as the post hospital for a time. Its three-storey octagonal tower was added in 1897 to act as an operating room; the shape helped to maximise natural light in an era when electricity still wasn't commonplace.
Funston Avenue, 94118

①

Palace of Fine Arts, Marina District
Permanently attractive

Like a fantasy of classical
antiquity, the Palace of Fine Arts
was built by beaux arts disciple
Bernard R Maybeck for the 1915
Panama-Pacific International
Exposition. While a crowning jewel
in a newly confident city, like the
other fair buildings it wasn't meant
to be permanent.

Maybeck wanted the site to fall
into gentle ruin but the city grew
attached to it and restoration work
turned it into a lasting structure –
meaning partially demolishing and
then rebuilding the original – in the
1960s. Today it holds concerts and
performances (*see page 94*).
3301 Lyon Street, 94123
palaceoffinearts.org

④
City Hall, Civic Center
Centre of excellence

This beaux arts centrepiece of San Francisco's "City Beautiful" movement occupies an entire block. The original building was destroyed by the 1906 earthquake and rebuilt for the 1915 Panama-Pacific International Exposition, designed by architect Arthur Brown Jr.

Noteworthy for the gilding on its impressive dome and around the main doors and balconies, the structure's aura of mightiness is enhanced by the towering lamps and pensive-looking carved men that form part of its columns.
1 Dr Carlton B Goodlett Place, 94102
sfgov.org

②
Hallidie Building, Financial District
Gilt-edged design

Home to the San Francisco chapter of the American Institute of Architects, the Hallidie Building is a real jaw-dropper. The façade is undoubtedly its most arresting feature. Designed by Willis Polk and built in 1917, its glass front (widely thought to be the first used in the US) makes it seem like a precursor to modern architecture.

What makes this building unique – and unlike more minimalist, modern structures – however are the flourishes on the exterior. The gothic cornice that sits alongside the metalwork on the fire escapes and railings in fact feels very art nouveau.
130 Sutter Street, 94104

③
Coit Tower, Telegraph Hill
Landmark bequest

A melding of classical architecture and art deco, Coit Tower sits atop the green peak of Telegraph Hill known as Pioneer Park. Built in 1933 at the bequest of a certain Lillie Hitchcock Coit, it was designed by Henry Howard, working for Arthur Brown Jr's firm (the same company behind the beaux arts city hall and opera house).

Some 65-metres tall, it tapers slightly at the apex to avoid looking top-heavy. It also features great views and beautiful murals.
1 Telegraph Hill Boulevard, 94133
+1 415 249 0995
sfrecpark.org

⑤
Eng-Skell Building, Soma
In good company

This building is a fine example of corporate heritage. Known today as Esco Foods, the Eng-Skell company decided in 1930 – three decades after it was founded – to build itself a grand HQ, designed by AC Griewank.

It's essentially a 9,000 sq m warehouse but with art deco trimmings: stepped, fluted pilasters stand by the doorway and divide the building into sections; and the roof features beautiful details such as a stepped triangular parapet. All this while retaining an industrial feel.
1043 Howard Street, 94103

Residential round-up

01 **Yerba Buena Lofts, Soma:** One of the most outstanding contemporary residential buildings to have emerged in San Francisco in recent years, this cube-like structure – with plenty of exposed concrete – is located in Soma and was designed by Stanley Saitowitz and his Natoma Architects firm. *855 Folsom Street, 94107*

02 **Feusier Octagon House, Russian Hill:** An offshoot of Victorian architecture, residential homes built on an octagonal plan are rare in San Francisco. They were the height of fashion in the 19th century, however, and this one was built in the mid-1850s; about 100 are thought to survive across the US. *1067 Green Street, 94133*

03 **Russell House, Presidio Heights:** Modernist residential buildings aren't as common here as they are in southern California and something about the 1951 Russell House – designed by Erich Mendelsohn – feels a little Los Angeles. It's worth a visit even though the view from the street is partial. *3788 Washington Street, 94118*

⑥
Sentinel Building, Financial District
One to watch out for

Compared with the neighbouring Transamerica Pyramid (*see page 113*), which was completed in 1972 and designed to be the height of modernity, the Sentinel (also known as Columbus Tower) is clearly from a different era entirely. Designed by Salfield & Kohlberg, its construction began before the 1906 quake and was finished the following year.

A beaux arts, flatiron-style building, it's clad in white tiles and copper that has turned an oxidised green. It has been owned by film-maker Francis Ford Coppola since 1972.
916 Kearny Street, 94133
+1 415 291 1700

Golden oldie

Mission San Francisco de Asis, also known as Mission Dolores, is the oldest, still-standing building in San Francisco, dating from 1776. The small white building is the surviving adobe structure. *missiondolores.org/64*

Lobbies
Foyer delight and delectation

(1)
111 Sutter Street, Financial District
Marvel at the marble

Also known as the Hunter-Dulin
Building, this French-style
romanesque structure from the
1920s was designed by New
Yorkers Schultze & Weaver and
was the West Coast headquarters
for the National Broadcasting
Company between 1927 and 1942.
   Restored at the end of the
millennium, the outside may look
a little like a faux French château
but the lobby is magnificent. With
enough marble to give Trump
Tower a run for its money, there
are beautiful frescoes of strutting
peacocks and floral motifs on the
ceiling to help transport you back
to a more opulent age.
111 Sutter Street, 94104

(2)
140 New Montgomery, Soma
Raising the roof

One of the city's great historic
tower blocks, this building designed
by Timothy Pflueger was opened
by the Pacific Telephone &
Telegraph Company in 1925
and features eight terracotta
eagles perched on its roof.
   A recent refurbishment and
seismic retrofit, costing tens of
millions of dollars, has kept all the
gothic-inspired art deco features
while adding a sculpture garden.
The metalwork around the lifts and
doors is beautiful but the highlight
is the lobby ceiling, inspired by
a Chinese brocade and featuring
everything from clouds to unicorns.
140 New Montgomery Street, 94105
140nm.com

③
Shell Building, Financial District
Gothic influences

Named for the petroleum company that used to occupy it, this building still has the corporation's logo engraved into the external cornice and on the floor of the heavily polished lobby. Designed by George Kelham and built in 1929, it's a magnificent example of the art deco office block.

The tower – like others in cities spanning Chicago, New York and Detroit – is thought to have been inspired by a stepped, gothic-influenced 1922 design from famed Finish-American Eliel Saarinen, which was once entered into a Chicago design competition but never saw the light of day.
100 Bush Street, 94104

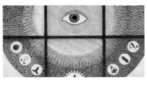

①
The Masonic, Nob Hill
Multiple murals

With its thin, towering columns and windowless approach (aside from the lobby), the 1958 Masonic (*see page 93*) has a brutalist feel. A frieze by Californian artist Emile Norman on the façade shows 3.7-metre figures representing the armed forces, as well as 14 marble figures in a tug-of-war (the struggle between good and evil).

Inside, the lobby features another Norman piece (his largest): an "endomosaic" mural that uses gravel and soil from all 58 counties in California to depict Masonic history.
1111 California Street, 94108
+1 415 776 7457
sfmasonic.com

②
One Bush Plaza, Financial District
Glass act

One Bush Plaza – also known as the Crown Zellerbach Building – epitomises the International Style of modernism, which did away with ornamentation and celebrated open spaces and the triple wonders of glass, concrete and steel.

Built in 1957 by architecture firm Skidmore, Owings & Merrill, it was the first glass curtain-wall skyscraper in San Francisco – the Hallidie Building had the first glass façade (*see page 108*) – and was built in its own private plaza. The building is perched on pillar supports that accentuate the floor-to-ceiling glass of the lobby.
1 Bush Street, 94104

③
The Cathedral of Saint Mary of the
Assumption, Fillmore District
Breathtaking spectacle

Located on a raised strip on the
edge of Japantown, this church is
incongruous with its surroundings
– but not in a bad way. The beauty
and spectacle of the structure
speak for themselves and the sheer
space that the building commands
is remarkable, including a paved
concrete approach that conjures
Brasília-meets-Tiananmen Square.

Built in 1971 and designed by
Italian modernist grandfathers
Pietro Belluschi and Pier Luigi
Nervi, its hyperbolic paraboloid
(really) roof sweeps towards the
sky. Look out, too, for the vast
pylons supporting the cupola, the
stained glass windows and a kinetic
sculpture by Richard Lippold
dangling above the altar. Truly
breathtaking, both inside and out.
1111 Gough Street, 94109
+1 415 567 2020
stmarycathedralsf.org

④
Transamerica Pyramid,
Financial District
Pyramid scheme

Originally home to the finance and
insurance company that gives it its
name, this tower was completed in
1972. It was designed by William
Pereira after Transamerica's
president John R Beckett noticed
that tall trees allow light to trickle
through – and why couldn't a high-
rise do the same?

The tallest building in the city
until the Salesforce Tower came
along, the pyramid gets its colour
from a coat of crushed white
quartz. As for the aluminium spike
at the top, it's actually hollow and
has a stairway inside it.
600 Montgomery Street, 94111
+1 415 829 5423

*See you at the
tip of the pyramid!*

⑤
PG&E Mission Substation, Soma
Shockingly good

Two things: first, this is indeed an
electric power station (well, a place
to house electric transformers, to
be precise) and, yes, we're aware
that's not exactly sexy. Second, it's
not situated in the loveliest part of
San Francisco for a jaunt (it's on
the edge of the Tenderloin).

That said, there's something
rather captivating about this most
utilitarian of buildings, which
despite its functional purpose
strives to be anything but boring.
Dating back to 1948, it has a
striking, almost Soviet feel to it,
thanks to the bas-relief murals
("Power and Light" by artist
Robert B Howard) on the side of
the building. Amendments to the
structure to secure and protect the
alcoves – such as a row of curved
steel – actually work pretty well too,
as does the uplighting.
1200-1236 Mission Street, 94103

**Privately owned public open
spaces (Popos)**

01 **Sansome Rooftop Deck,
Financial District:** Head
straight through the lobby
and up to the 15th floor,
where you'll find tables
and chairs, geometric tiles
and a colourful central
sundial shaped like an
obelisk. As for the views?
They don't get much better
than an eyeful of the
Transamerica Pyramid.
222 Halleck Alley, 94129

02 **One Kearny Rooftop,
Financial District:** Tell
security you're there to
view the roof and you're in
(just remember to bring ID).
The 11th-floor space offers
great views in the heart of
downtown. Note that it
only opens from 10.00 to
17.00, Monday to Friday
(though you can also rent
it for a private party).
onekearnyclub.com

03 **555 Mission Sculpture
Garden, South Beach:**
This ground-level sculpture
garden was designed by
Hargreaves Associates.
Don't miss Swiss artist
Ugo Rondinone's playful
head sculptures or
Jonathan Borofsky's
"Human Structures",
62 painted-steel figures,
linked to form a tower.
555 Mission Street, 94105

Old and new
———
Studio Libeskind designed the
extension of the Contemporary
Jewish Museum (*see page 94*).
Worth seeing if only for the
juxtaposition between the blue,
steel-clad angles of the former
and the 19th-century red-
brick structure of the latter
(a former power plant).
thecjm.org

Contemporary
Up-to-date attractions

① De Young Museum, Golden
Gate Park
Building regeneration

This museum has known several
guises since its initial construction
in 1894. Originally the Fine Arts
Building, it was damaged in
1906 and reworked in an ornate
Spanish plateresque style, with the
addition of a tower and west wing.
After the quake in 1989, it was a
decade before a privately financed
institution was built from a design
by Swiss firm Herzog & de Meuron.

The result is a copper shell –
complete with wood and stone
– with perforated holes that
keep the treetops visible through
windows. The 44-metre tower is
also mighty impressive.
*50 Hagiwara Tea Garden Drive,
94118
+1 415 750 3600
deyoung.famsf.org*

② San Francisco Federal Building,
Soma
Open government

An example of deconstructivism –
the postmodern ethos of building
on fragmented parts (the Walt
Disney Concert Hall in LA is a
prime example) – the 18-storey
Federal Building opened in 2007.

Designed by Thom Mayne
(founder of LA firm Morphosis),
the building is a thin form made of
perforated metal, which changes
according to the angle from which
you see it. With outdoor benches
and a public café, it's both an
imposing mark of officialdom
and an attempt to make a federal
building more open – no easy task
in an age of heightened security.
90 7th Street, 94103

③

Congregation Beth Sholom,
Inner Richmond
A very modern synagogue

In the residential Inner Richmond
there's a row of neat and tidy
townhouses from before the
Second World War. And then there's
something very different too: what
looks like a concrete ship's hull –
or the curve of a menorah.

This contemporary synagogue
(which could admittedly do with a
bit of a clean-up) was completed in
2008. The yellow concrete sitting
on zinc-plated aluminium panels
was designed by Stanley Saitowitz
from Natoma Architects, which
also designed the city's Yerba
Buena Lofts (*see page 109*).
301 14th Avenue, 94118
+1 415 221 8736

④

Ray and Dagmar Dolby
Regeneration Medicine Building,
Forest Knolls
Campus shake-up

Part of the University of California
at San Francisco's Parnassus
campus, this building was designed
by Rafael Viñoly Architects (the
firm behind Oxford's Mathematical
Institute and the extensions to
the Rockefeller University in
New York).

The pointed structure, clad in
corrugated steel, follows the curve
of the hillside and is kept sturdy by
space trusses that act as legs and
seismic base isolators (this is San
Francisco, after all). There's also a
lush rooftop garden for employees.
505 Parnassus Avenue, 9413
ucsf.edu

①
Signage
Attention grabbers

San Francisco may not be as inundated with signs as, say, Las Vegas or Miami but look in the right spots and you'll find some real beauties. One of the most instantly recognisable is the vibrant Britex Fabrics sign, just off Union Square, a San Francisco institution since 1952.

There's also some classic neon on display, from the cocktail glass of High Tide in the Tenderloin to 500 Club in the Mission (another cocktail glass) and the rather more kitsch Owl Tree (you guessed it). The sign for Tony's Cable Car Restaurant is also fun, as is the New Mission Alamo cinema. We could go on and on.

2
F-line historic trams
Streetcars to desire

San Francisco has operated its cable cars continuously since 1873 but its trams have fared less well, losing out to buses. Aside from a comeback in 1982, when the cable-car system was being redone, the best trams got was a run out for a series of summer festivals.

In 1995, however, their rebirth was secured with the F-line: historic trams from around the US and further afield, decked out in the colours of their native cities. Many are the beautiful art deco PCCs (Presidents' Conference Committees) that were rolled out in the 1930s. A great heritage project that has proven popular with both tourists and San Franciscans alike.

③
Sutro Tower
Get the picture?

San Franciscans didn't exactly warm to this colossal antenna tower when it first showed up in 1972 to better TV reception in the area. Designed by AC Martin & Associates and visible all around the city thanks to its lofty position, it's particularly dramatic when there's fog hovering in the vicinity.

These days it's undoubtedly a San Francisco landmark. And that red-and-white colouring? Dictated by aviation regulations to avert plane collisions.

4
Secret stairways
Step to it

When city blueprints were drafted in the 19th century, property developers pressured civil engineer Jasper O'Farrell to discard his plans to weave around the hills and instead divide the city in a grid. This resulted in properties being perched atop hills far too steep for paved roads and horse-drawn carriages.

The answer? Stairways were installed to aid the final climb, often from the backs of neighbours' gardens. Even today these hidden, wonky steps remain the only access route for some residents to reach their homes.

Sport and fitness
—— Active options

Studded with parks and fringed by beaches and the waters of the bay, San Francisco attracts many who simply want to enjoy its considerable natural attributes. And given that San Franciscans are an active bunch too, you can expect to see them out in droves, whether running, cycling or surfing. Even a walk in the park can be something special, given the dramatic views on offer.

There is, however, a flipside to all this: now and again, the weather will let you down. Chilly, rolling fog tends to take the fun out of even the most appealing outdoor activity. But never fear, there's plenty to keep you busy indoors too, from pounding punchbags at a boxing gym to channelling the 1980s at a roller disco. You can even give your wits a workout at the oldest chess club in the US.

And, of course, when it's time to unwind, follow our directions to some of the city's best grooming and spa offerings. A fine end to a full day.

①
Surfing
Catch a wave

Despite notoriously chilly water and the occasional shark sighting, San Francisco's surf scene is one of the best in the country. Decent spots dot the coast both north and south of the city and boast everything from beach breaks for beginners to the legendary Mavericks for big-wave surfers.

It's important to pick a patch that matches your abilities, so be sure to do your research. If you're in any doubt, get in touch with one of the city's surf schools for a lesson. Or simply experience the surf without getting wet: watching locals catch waves from Fort Point can be almost as fun as being out there yourself. Almost.

1

3rd Street Boxing Gym, Dogpatch
Knockout workouts

Come to 3rd Street ready to sweat.
Classes here range from cardio
boxing to full boxing lessons with
former pros such as Ed Gutierrez.
There's even a class to help control
the effects of Parkinson's disease.
   "We want to make sure that
our workouts are harder, better
and stronger than anywhere else
in the city," says general manager
Cameron Wisdom.
2576 3rd Street, 94107
+1 415 550 8269
3rdstreetboxing.com

2

Dolores Park, Dolores Heights
Holding court

A favourite place for lounging in
the sun with a view of the city,
Dolores Park also has great
facilities for more active pursuits.
   Six superbly surfaced tennis
courts at the park's northern
edge offer a great spot for a knock
around, while just beside them is
a full basketball court for hoop-
shooters. Since the Golden State
Warriors have been wiping the
floor with their NBA competition,
basketball has become big in
San Francisco. This is where
you'll see aspiring ballplayers
of all ages working on their best
Steph Curry jumpshots.
Dolores Street & 19th Street, 94114
+1 415 554 9521

More outdoor activities

01 Archery: Let fly with the
San Francisco Archers:
BYO bow and arrows
or pop by an outreach
session on the first and
third Sundays of the
month for a lesson.
sfarchers.org

02 Cycling: The Bay Area's
hilly and scenic roads
make for excellent rides.
The San Francisco Cycling
Club goes out every
weekday, in the city or on
the peninsula headlands.
sfcyclingclub.org

3

The South End Rowing Club,
Fisherman's Wharf
Take to the water

The South End Rowing Club is a
San Francisco institution. Founded
in 1873 strictly for rowing, it now
covers open-water swimming,
running and handball too. Club
members have competed in the
Olympics, swum the English
Channel and swim from Alcatraz
to San Francisco without wetsuits
(*see page 81*).
   It's not all business though: good
food, drink and parties are just as
much part of the club's identity.
After all, its unofficial motto is "To
be a South Ender is to love life".
500 Jefferson Street, 94109
+1 415 776 7372
serc.com

I can do that,
no problem!

Studiomix, Tenderloin
Vary your training

Studiomix is a far cry from your typical gym. As its name suggests, the philosophy here is to shake up standard gym routines with considered coaching and upbeat music.

The independent fitness studio and full-service health club offers everything from rock climbing (there's a three-storey indoor rock wall) and barre to spinning and martial arts. All of the above take place in 2,800 sq m of bright, roomy and modern studio space in Little Saigon.
1000 Van Ness Avenue, 94109
+1 415 926 6790
studiomix.com

③
Mechanics' Institute Chess Room, Financial District
Pawn stars

The oldest chess club in the US, the Mechanics' Institute Chess Room opened in 1854 as a meeting place for employees of the city's mechanical industries.

Housed in a grand clubhouse that was built after the 1906 earthquake, the chess room is open to guests and hosts events and tournaments all year round; the weekly highlight is the Tuesday Night Marathon, which attracts players of all ages, backgrounds and levels of experience.
57 Post Street, 94104
+1 415 393 0110
chessclub.org

②
Church of 8 Wheels, Lower Haight
Roll with it

Built in 1897, the Italianate Sacred Heart Church was one of the city's grandest places of worship. It survived both the 1906 and 1989 quakes but by 2004, attendance had dwindled and the church fell into disrepair.

Enter David Miles Jr, the "godfather of skate" and a regular at the Sunday rollerskating sessions in Golden Gate Park. He transformed the space into a roller disco – home to the Holy Rollers dance troupe – and it's been a sanctuary to those seeking roller-salvation on Friday and Saturday nights ever since.
554 Fillmore Street, 94117
+1 415 752 1967
churchof8wheels.com

I told you I could do more than downward-facing dog

Grooming and spas
Keeping trim

①
JP Kempt Barber & Social,
Lower Haight
Vanity flair

Shorty Maniace has run
barbershops in New York
and Seattle but after working
independently in San Francisco,
he decided to make the city his
home and opened JP Kempt
Barber & Social in 2013.

All the haircuts, hot-lather beard
trims and straight-razor shaves a
man could want are available in this
chic but casual setting. Take a seat
in one of the old-fashioned chairs
and admire the products on show
in the glass-fronted oak vanities.
351 Divisadero Street, 94117
+1 415 437 1300
jpkempt.com

②
International Orange Spa,
Pacific Heights
Bright idea

The goal at International Orange
Spa – the name is taken from the
colour of paint used on the Golden
Gate Bridge (*see page 103*) – is to
offer a break from the pressures
of everyday urban life. The bright
interiors are warm and welcoming,
with leafy pot plants and plenty
of wood.

Restorative yoga classes and
acupuncture are on the menu,
along with more traditional spa
treatments such as massages
and facials.
2044 Fillmore Street, 94115
+1 415 563 5000
internationalorange.com

③
Veer & Wander, Hayes Valley
Open to all

Hairstylist Connie McGrath
opened Veer & Wander in 2013
and it has already become a staple
among San Francisco's growing
number of salons that offer cuts
for both men and women.

It's more than just a place to
get your hair done, though: Veer
& Wander is also an apothecary
of sorts and stocks numerous
grooming products, including clay
facemasks by Clark's Botanicals
and room fragrances by Echo
Park's Sandoval.
6 Brady Street, 94103
+1 415 864 3012
veerandwander.com

Parks
Wide open spaces

①

Grandview Park, Inner Sunset
Neighbourhood high point

This aptly named park has a 360-degree view of the city from downtown to Port Reyes and over to Lake Merced. It was created by sand dunes drifting over 140 million-year-old rock but urbanisation in the 1940s cut it off from replenishing coastal sand; stick to the paths to limit erosion and protect the endangered plants.

The most picturesque access to the 3km of trails is via a mosaic staircase made by local residents on Moraga and 14th.
Moraga Street and 14th
Avenue, 94122
+1 415 831 5500
sfrecpark.org/destination/
grand-view-park

---

②

The Presidio, Presidio
Military base turned outdoor space

Starting out as a Spanish fort in 1776, The Presidio was next manned by Mexicans and then the US Army from 1846. When the army left in 1994, the 600-hectare space (that's about 5 per cent of the city) became a national park.

There are scenic viewpoints aplenty and the grassy expanse of the Main Parade Ground is perfect for a picnic. Nature-lovers should visit Crissy Marsh, reclaimed military land that's now home to some 100 bird species and 110 varieties of native flora.
Visitor centre: 210 Lincoln
Boulevard, 94129
+1 415 561 4323
presidio.gov

Hiking

01 Marin Headlands: On the other side of the Golden Gate Bridge, the Marin Headlands have a variety of trails taking in cliffside rocks, serene woodlands and pebbled beaches. Take the Point Bonita Trail up to the Lighthouse or the easier Rodeo Lagoon Trail, ending with a picturesque ocean view.

02 Twin Peaks: Tackle this hike on a sunny day to be treated to the grandest view of San Francisco. The trail is just over a kilometre long and rises to a height of 281 metres, where there are spectacular panoramic views of the Bay Area and beyond.

③
Golden Gate Park
Main attraction

With some 13 million visitors each year, this is the third most-visited park in the US. The crown jewel among the city's 220 public green spaces, it was founded in 1871 by engineer William Hammond Hall and master gardener John McLaren.

Beyond the regular trees, plants and streets of a park, the features here range from the California Academy of Science and Dutch windmills to an archery field and summer festivals. Tour the area by foot, bike or rollerblades.
Lincoln Way or Fulton Street, 94122
+1 415 831 5520
goldengatepark.com

Get a wiggle on

On a map, the zig-zagging cycle path known as The Wiggle seems a horrendously inconvenient way in which to travel around the Lower Haight. Once you're on it, however, the reason behind it is immediately evident: it dodges the city's notoriously leg-busting hills.

Beaches
Make the most of the coast

Tipping point
This is the city's southernmost beach

❶
Fort Funston, Lakeshore
Take a hike

Part of the Golden Gate National Recreation Area, Fort Funston beach caters to just about everyone. Hikers and horseriders can choose from plentiful trails – including one to Battery Davis, a base for 16-inch guns during the Second World War – while the paved loop walks are suited to wheelchair access. It's also one of the best places for exercising the dog, sans lead.

The chief drawcard for many, however, is the 60-metre-tall bluffs. Coupled with the brisk winds, they make this a hang-gliding hotspot.
Fort Funston Road, 94101
+1 415 561 4323
parksconservancy.org/visit/park-sites/
fort-funston.html

Eyes front

The north of
Baker Beach
is "clothing
optional"

②
Baker Beach, Presidio
With the grain

A stone's throw from Golden Gate
Bridge and running along the
western edge of The Presidio park,
San Francisco's large Baker Beach
is often packed on warm weekends,
with everyone from CrossFit
enthusiasts to sun seekers.

History buffs can check out the
"disappearing gun" – a 45-tonne
cannon that's cranked in and out
of hiding – and there's also a picnic
area and access to the Coastal Trail
for hikers. Be aware that swimming
here is unsafe thanks to the large
waves and strong currents.
1504 Pershing Drive, 94129
+1 415 561 4323
parksconservancy.org/visit/park-sites/
baker-beach.html

③
Ocean Beach, Outer Richmond
and Outer Sunset
Go to great lengths

Taking in the city's entire western
edge, Ocean Beach is almost 5km
long. But given its urban location
it's remarkably free from crowds
(except on the hottest days).

Surfers are the only people who
venture into the water – dangerous
rips in places mean it's not ideal
for swimming – while cyclists and
walkers can enjoy the esplanade
at the top end. The black sections
of the beach are the result of
magnetite rock washing up here.
Great Highway (start at Point
Lobos Avenue), 94121
+1 415 561 4323
parksconservancy.org/visit/park-sites/
ocean-beach.html

Spectator sports

01 NFL: The San Francisco
49ers were founded in
1946 and the team is one
of the most recognisable
and lucrative football
franchises in the US.
The home stadium is in
Santa Clara, having
moved from Candlestick
Park in 2014.
49ers.com

02 Baseball: The San
Francisco Giants' home
ground (AT&T Park) is
one of the most evocative
sports arenas in the
US. Few other sporting
contests unfold against
a backdrop like San
Francisco Bay.
mlb.com/giants

03 Basketball: The Golden
State Warriors, who
moved to the Bay Area
from Philadelphia in 1962,
boast one of the city's
most recognisable logos:
a yellow depiction of the
Bay bridge against a
royal-blue background.
nba.com/warriors

Cycling route
Saddle up

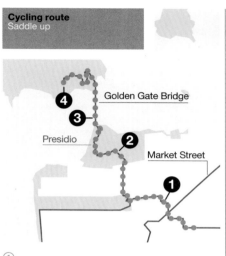

Golden Gate Bridge

Presidio

Market Street

Running route
Pavement pounding

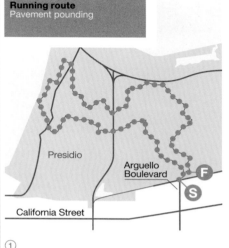

Presidio

Arguello Boulevard

California Street

---

① Golden Gate Bridge
Marathon effort

This ride takes you from the Mission District, across the iconic bridge to Marin County, and back.

STARTING POINT: 21st Street, Mission District
DISTANCE: 35km

This ride is serious business and most cyclists set off pre-dawn to avoid the heat and ensure that they're back in time for work (it takes about 2.5 hours to complete). Consider joining a peloton dispatching from Mission Cycling on 21st Street.

Take the green bike lanes out of the Mission, crossing Market Street and following ❶ *The Wiggle*. This clearly signed trail helps you dodge the hills and lands you on Fell Street. Head west then cut through Golden Gate Park to reach Arguello Boulevard and ride it through Inner Richmond to the ❷ *Presidio*. Once in the national park, follow Arguello, which turns into Washington and then Lincoln Boulevard. Pay attention here: to land yourself on the ❸ *Golden Gate Bridge*, you need to go under the highway then immediately turn left, left again and then right.

Once across and on the shores of Marin County, take the Alexander Avenue exit and loop left, then turn right on Conzelman Road. Now's the hard part: the next 2.5km are a gradual 150-metre climb but the road hugs the coastline so the views are spectacular and the breeze (as long as it's not a gale) is rather cooling. Weave your way up the hill and take the second exit at the roundabout to continue on Conzelman. As you near the top, the road swings around to the right and there's a carpark for ❹ *Marin Headlands Vista Point*. Pull in and soak up the view across the bay to San Francisco. All that's left to do now is cycle back; luckily you have an easy glide downhill to kickstart the return.

---

① Presidio
Military manoeuvres

DISTANCE: 8.3km
GRADIENT: Some steep inclines
DIFFICULTY: Moderate
HIGHLIGHT: View of the Golden Gate Bridge
BEST TIME: Early morning
NEAREST STATION: California Street and Arguello Boulevard bus stop

This run loops through the former army base and past what's probably the best view of the Golden Gate Bridge. Enter via the Arguello Gate and take the Bay Area Ridge Trail that forks off to your left. In the clearing is Andy Goldsworthy's "Spire" sculpture, installed in 2008 as a symbol of reforestation.

Continue through the woods and at the junction take the lower track to your right, which merges with Washington Boulevard. Take the next right, Nauman Road, to enjoy the view from the *National Cemetery Overlook*. Continue along the Bay Area Ridge Trail, cross Park Boulevard and continue through the woods to emerge on Central Magazine Road. At the T-junction, turn left on Washington before leaving the road at *Immigrant Point* to head down the stairs, following the signs to the Batteries to Bluffs Trail. It's here that you'll enjoy a view of the Golden Gate Bridge.

Pass Battery Godfrey and, just before the carpark, cut right to cross Lincoln Boulevard and run alongside *Fort Winfield Scott*. Pass the flagpole and turn right, then left on Kobbe Avenue to pass the officers' residences. Run under Highway 1 and, when the roads split, continue straight to join the Park Trail. Turn right onto Presidio Promenade Trail and right again onto Sheridan Avenue, passing the *Presidio Officers' Club*. Take a final right onto Funston Avenue and you'll find the Ecology Trail, which will take you back to the start.

Walks
—— Take to the streets

It's possible that the word "walk", when used in conjunction with San Francisco, will fill you with dread. No one wants to drag themselves up and down all those hills, right?

In fact, this is one of the most walkable cities in the US and to pass up the chance to explore it on foot is to pass up the chance to experience its neighbourhoods at their best. These rambles will put you right in the thick of things, without straining your legs *too* much.

NEIGHBOURHOOD 01

Outer Sunset
Coastal calm

If San Francisco seems more town than city, then the Outer Sunset will make you feel like you've stumbled into a laidback beachside village quite removed from the big smoke. It's hard to believe that this neighbourhood, gazing out at the Pacific on the city's western edge, is just a short car ride away from the relatively hectic confines of downtown. Previously known as "Carville" (it was once a dumping ground for old railcars that were often turned into homes), the area now retains a strong sense of community despite a few hints at changing currents.

Set out on a grid of hilly streets – the first letter of each streetname follows an alphabetical order, while the avenues are numbered – there's a wistful, creative vibe to the neighbourhood that's utterly alluring. And while you could easily just plonk yourself on the (albeit slightly breezy) beach and take in the scenic beauty of northern California, there's plenty for you to explore in the backstreets too. What's more, there's no shortage of time for a chat in a community where people tend to know each other's first names – indeed, the Outer Sunset is perennially unflustered. So stroll with us as we visit a garage that doubles as a ceramics studio, sample coffee and something stiffer at a dive bar, and take in a few more retail and food options while we're at it.

[Map showing Outer Sunset walk with Golden Gate Park, Irving Street, Judah Street, N-Judah, Lawton Street, Gulf of the Farallones, Noriega Street, 47th Avenue, 43rd Avenue, Taraval Street, and numbered stops 1–12]

Laidback lifestyle
Outer Sunset walk

Start the walk where Golden Gate Park meets Lincoln Way and Great Highway (there's a boardwalk looking down onto the beach), checking out the early 20th-century Dutch windmills on the western fringes of the park.

Head east on Lincoln until 47th and turn right to reach number 1235; there's a banner outside and the garage door is normally open. It's from here that **1** *Outer Sunset*

Pottery operates. Owner Larry Letofsky's pieces are sold in local shops but buy directly from him and you'll get to hear about his love of jazz while flicking through his library of books on pottery greats.

After a chinwag, continue south on 47th to Irving Street and hang a left. About half a block up on the right is 2 *3 Fish Studios*, a fun spot selling prints that can be framed on site. The affable owner Eric Rewitzer – whose California bear print has been ordered by several Democratic Californian senators – may even offer you a pint of Anchor stout from a tap out back. Almost opposite is 3 *Mollusk Surf Shop* (*see page 48*), a great place to get a T-shirt or even a board.

Continue up the hill and on your right between 45th and 44th you'll see exhibition space 4 *Irving Street Projects*. Hours aren't regular so check in advance if you'd like a tour. Head halfway between 43rd and 42nd and visit 5 *Avenues Dry Goods* on the left. Here you can pick up everything from a tea towel to a rug, most likely made by local designers.

Getting there

The N-Judah light rail runs from downtown to Ocean Beach. Alternatively take a taxi or hop on a bike and cycle through Golden Gate Park (highly recommended). You'll find bike rentals from Parkwide at the east end of the park on Stanyan Street.

Walk back the way you came and turn left down 43rd then right on Judah Street, which has a cluster of great places to visit. The jewel in the crown is 6 *Outerlands* (*see page 25*) on the corner of 45th. The wood-dominated restaurant serves comforting fodder (think salmon with black-eyed peas and harissa) and also bakes some of the finest bread in town. If it's too busy, continue on the left side of Judah to 7 *Woods Outbound*, a minimalist space to top up your beer levels and wash down some empanadas. Almost next door is 8 *Case for Making*, a shop that sells everything from magazines to its own watercolours.

Retrace your steps, stopping in at General Store (*see page 51*), and turn right down 43rd. Keep walking for a few blocks past the colourful houses and you'll soon reach the beautiful art deco Francis Scott Key School on the corner of Kirkham Street. Continue to Lawton Street and you'll find 9 *Andytown Coffee Roasters*, an excellent pit-stop for a caffeine fix.

On the same block is 10 *The Great Highway Gallery* (closed on Sundays), which focuses on contemporary art. Next door, peek into 11 *Lawton Tap Room*, which sells locally brewed beers and Mexican food, should you have any room left. If you're still kicking after all that, take a slow stagger – it's about a 20-minute walk – south down 43rd until you reach Taraval Street. Now turn right and walk towards the ocean. Just before 47th you'll arrive at your final stop, 12 *The Riptide*, a wood-panelled, no-frills bar that's the local hangout of choice.

Address book

01 **Outer Sunset Pottery**
1235 47th Avenue, 94122
letofskystudio.net

02 **3 Fish Studios**
4541 Irving Street, 94122
+1 415 242 3474
3fishstudios.com

03 **Mollusk Surf Shop**
4500 Irving Street, 94122
+1 415 564 6300
mollusksurfshop.com

04 **Irving Street Projects**
4331 Irving Street, 94122
irvingstreetprojects.org

05 **Avenues Dry Goods**
4120 Irving Street, 94122
+1 415 841 2870
avenuesdrygoods.com

06 **Outerlands**
4001 Judah Street, 94122
+1 415 661 6140
outerlandssf.com

07 **Woods Outbound**
4045 Judah Street, 94122
+1 415 571 8025
woodsbeer.com/outbound

08 **Case for Making**
4037 Judah Street, 94122
caseformaking.com

09 **Andytown Coffee Roasters**
3655 Lawton Street, 94122
+1 415 753 9775
andytownsf.com

10 **The Great Highway Gallery**
3649 Lawton Street, 94122
+1 415 680 3891
thegreathighway.com

11 **Lawton Tap Room**
3645 Lawton Street, 94122
+1 415 340 3654
sevenstillsofsf.com/pages/lawton-tap-room

12 **The Riptide**
639 Taraval Street, 94116
+1 415 681 8433
riptidesf.com

NEIGHBOURHOOD 02
Dogpatch
Industrial artland

Dogpatch may seem a charming name, until a San Franciscan recalls its origins: years ago, so the story goes, the streets of the neighbourhood were patrolled by packs of strays roaming between slaughterhouses in search of meat scraps.

It may not be an appealing tale but it speaks of the area's industrial past. Broad tributaries of bitumen intersect blocks of warehouses that show the strain of decades of shipbuilding, butchery and train mechanics. Among them are short strips of Victorian-era houses where workers lived; one of the best preserved areas is down 22nd Street and the blocks just north of it, which were lucky enough to survive the 1906 earthquake.

Today these houses form the nucleus of an art and retail hub born when food enthusiasts Sher Rogat and Margherita Stewart Sagan opened their restaurant Piccino in 2006. The change was by no means rapid although artists and craftsmen were already based in the area; the real catalyst came with an influx of retailers from 2011. Patron of the arts Ann Hatch opened Workshop Residence, fashion heavyweights Ben and Chris Ospital opted to base their second outpost here, and others have trickled in since. The retailers, restaurants and galleries have multiplied and now extend beyond the workers' houses to the industrial blocks on Minnesota Street and the main drag of 3rd.

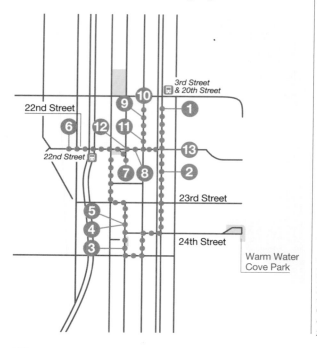

Urban revival
Dogpatch walk

Start the day at **1** *Neighbor Bakehouse* with a creamy flat white and what's surely one of the tastiest croissants this side of the pond. It's a Dogpatch mainstay so lines can be long but service is quick and friendly. Go south on 3rd Street to visit the **2** *Museum of Craft and Design,* opened in 2004 as a non-collecting institution dedicated to both contemporary and modern designers, makers and artists.

Exit the museum and head south again, taking note of the odd mix across the road: a boxing gym, warehouses, barbers and shiny new apartment blocks. It's not that pretty but it's an interesting insight into how the population is sprawling into previously ignored areas.

Turn right on 24th and, when you reach Tennessee Street, turn left and then right on 25th. The way into your next stop is through the car park on 25th at the corner of Minnesota Street. The large hangar at the end is one of three spaces belonging to the Minnesota Street Project and home to commercial-art contender **3** *Adrian Rosenfeld Gallery.* A private collector has set up shop next door.

Return through the car park and walk north on Minnesota, passing the workshop and headquarters of womenswear label Tina Frey Designs. Cross the street and stop for lunch at **4** *Alta,* located inside the main site of **5** *Minnesota Street Project* (*see page 98*). This two-storey space

is home to 11 galleries, including Nancy Toomey Fine Art.

Exit and head north, passing the project's third space, dedicated to artists' studios, and then Thatcher's Gourmet Popcorn (hence the buttery smell). Turn left at the corner then right onto Indiana Street, passing the city's transport depot. At 22nd, turn left; this next strip was the starting point for the area's gentrification and is prettier than the surrounding streets. Continue your gallery hop at visual, installation and performance-art arbiter ❻ *Romer Young Gallery* then retrace your steps to the corner of 22nd and Indiana, and walk east through Woods Yard Park. At the yellow Victorian house (it dates from 1859) dip into the smaller outpost of Chris and Ben Ospital's Modern Appealing Clothing (*see page 47*). Also stop by old-time wine merchant ❼ *Dig* to snag a bottle.

Head back to 22nd. You'll pass Piccino on the corner (we'll be back) as you head east, stopping in at ❽ *Workshop Residence* (*see page 52*). Then take a left on Tennessee

Street to reach the cream-coloured building at number 1060: built in 1895, the former ❾ *Irving M Scott School* is the city's oldest public-school building still standing. At number 909, the 1925 ❿ *Fire Engine House No 16* was designed by city architect John Reid Jr and, while disbanded in 1970, is still owned by the city.

Return south to design shop ⓫ *Industrious Life*, which stocks contemporary US-made homeware and a few vintage finds. Hopefully you've worked up an appetite, so double back to ⓬ *Piccino* for farm-fresh Italian fare and an impeccable wine list. As for dessert, beeline east and cross 3rd to sample the ice cream at ⓭ *Mr and Mrs Miscellaneous*. Both pastry chefs, husband-and-wife duo Ian Flores and Annabelle Topacio opened the joint in 2010. Be sure to pick up some peanut brittle and sour cherry liquorice as take-homes.

Getting there

The heart of the neighbourhood on 22nd is straddled by the 22nd Street Station, serviced by the Caltrain line. The 3rd Street and 20th Street Station is serviced by the Sunnydale-bound T line on the Muni network and is opposite the starting point.

NEIGHBOURHOOD 03

North Beach
Eclectically old and new

A large portion of San Francisco was lost in the devastating 1906 earthquake and the culturally eclectic neighbourhood of North Beach was among the worst hit. Prior to this, it was known for being a small pocket of Italy while also serving as a neighbour to the bustling Chinatown; it was also recognised for its brothels, bars, jazz clubs and other underground vices that earned it the nickname The Barbary Coast. Following the quake however, big banks rolled in to stake their claims on well-positioned patches of land and chase out the area's taboo tenants. Flatiron-style banking institutions were erected alongside the Italian trattorias, some of which, including the Tosca Café and Fior d'Italia, are still open today.

By the 1950s, North Beach had undergone yet another iconic cultural shift and become synonymous with the US's Beat generation. The likes of Allen Ginsberg and Jack Kerouac were reciting their poetry at City Lights (*see page 60*), drawing in the bohemian crowd that led to the opening of cafés in the mould of Vesuvio Café and Caffe Trieste, as well as boutiques and theatres. This era continues to sway the neighbourhood, with comedy clubs, jazz bars and theatres operating into the early hours.

Retail and repasts
North Beach walk

Kick off your walk with some freshly baked focaccia from ① *Liguria Bakery*, the no-nonsense, family-owned *focacceria* that has been a North Beach fixture since 1911. Get there sooner rather than later because once they're sold out it's lights out, regardless of the time. Liguria isn't a sit-down establishment, so you'll need to take your fare diagonally across the street and set up a picnic at the charming ② *Washington Square Park*, home to Saints Peter and Paul Church. Find a bench or a patch of grass and ogle the massive, 58-metres-high bell towers. Originally constructed in 1884, the church was rebuilt in 1924, 18 years after being destroyed by the earthquake. It has also been a significant pop-culture icon, featuring in Clint Eastwood's films *Dirty Harry* and *The Dead Pool*.

When you're finished, head over to the park's northeast corner where Stockton Street and Filbert Street intersect. Walk

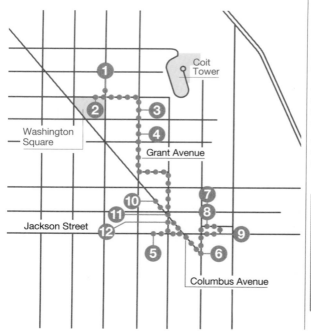

Getting there

Many bus lines – including the 8, 30, 39, 41 and 45 – stop close to Washington Square Park. Fortunately, once you're at the square, anywhere in North Beach is easily navigable, so use it as your drop-off and pick-up point.

Address book

01 **Liguria Bakery**
1700 Stockton Street, 94133
+1 415 421 3786

02 **Washington Square Park**
666 Filbert Street, 94133
+1 415 421 0809

03 **AB Fits**
1519 Grant Avenue, 94133
+1 415 982 5726
abfits.com

04 **101 Music**
1414 Grant Avenue, 94133
+1 415 392 6369

05 **Great Eastern**
649 Jackson Street, 94133
+1 415 986 2500
greateasternsf.com

06 **Church of Scientology**
701 Montgomery Street, 94111

07 **William Stout Architectural Books**
804 Montgomery Street, 94133
+1 415 391 6757
stoutbooks.com

08 **Gallery Japonesque**
824 Montgomery Street, 94133
+1 415 391 8860
japonesquegallery.com

09 **Guideboat Co**
441 Jackson Street, 94111
+1 415 649 6214
guideboat.com

10 **Tosca Café**
242 Columbus Avenue, 94133
+1 415 986 9651
toscacafesf.com

11 **Comstock Saloon**
155 Columbus Avenue, 94133
+1 415 617 0071
comstocksaloon.com

12 **Café Zoetrope**
916 Kearny Street, 94133
+1 415 291 1700
cafezoetrope.com

east on Filbert, then take a right on Grant Avenue to reach ③ *AB Fits*. This shop is a destination for denim-lovers; it specialises in repairs and customisation and has an impressive range of denim clothes for sale. Further along Grant Avenue is ④ *101 Music*, a hidden gem where you can pick up jazz, rock and rare vinyl. Exit and head further south, then turn left onto Fresno Street and continue until you reach Kearny. Make a right and head south until you reach Jackson Street then turn right again to arrive at ⑤ *Great Eastern* for a traditional Chinese lunch. After dim sum favoured by the likes of Barack Obama, head back east on Jackson Street and take the second right onto Columbus Avenue to reach the flatiron building that's now home to the ⑥ *Church of Scientology*. Following the earthquake of 1906, this building was constructed two storeys high as the Banca Popolare Italiana Operaia Fugazi. A third floor was added in 1916 and the building later housed the Bank of America.

Head north on Montgomery Street and peek into the charming ⑦ *William Stout Architectural Books* to preview a collection of rare and out-of-print publications. When you're done, walk about 25 metres to ⑧ *Gallery Japonesque*, where you can nosedive into the zeitgeist of contemporary Japanese artwork. Make a left when you exit to amble down the historic Gold Street and, about midway along, look out for an unmarked street to your right that looks about the size of a driveway. Take it back to Jackson Street to find ⑨ *Guideboat*

Co, which sells boats and nautical-inspired clothing.

Head west to Columbus Avenue to dine on pig tails and meatballs at ⑩ *Tosca Café (see page 33)*, an art deco trattoria revitalised by the team behind New York's The Spotted Pig. This favoured venue is soaked in San Francisco history. Afterwards, pop across the road to ⑪ *Comstock Saloon* for a classic drink and oysters if you didn't get your fill at dinner. If you're feeling adventurous, ask the bartender for the Barkeep's Whimsy but be warned – it packs a punch.

Finally, enjoy a tiramisu at ⑫ *Café Zoetrope* in the Sentinel Building *(see page 109)*, made popular by its owner, Francis Ford Coppola. Take your time and drink in the architecture: this is one of the only buildings on the route to have survived the great earthquake.

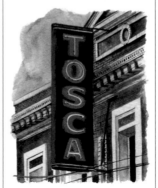

NEIGHBOURHOOD 04
The Castro
Variety show

Although the gay population of San Francisco began expanding during the Second World War, The Castro only blossomed as the hub of the gay and lesbian communities in the 1960s. The neighbourhood, wedged between the Mission and the Haight-Ashbury, was originally home to a large population of Swedish and Irish immigrants who arrived at the turn of the 20th century but the demographic shifted and gay-friendly bars such as The Missouri Mule and Lucky 13 opened on Market Street in the 1960s, attracting a young, liberal crowd.

The Castro rapidly became a thriving meeting point for those seeking political change and in the 1970s it was home to Harvey Milk, the first openly gay man to be elected to public office in California. On 27 November 1978, Milk was assassinated at city hall along with mayor George Moscone; The Castro became the focus of a community in grief, with renewed waves of activism after Milk's death. His name and image are still ubiquitous around the area, as is the rainbow flag painted onto the pedestrian crossings and draped from flagpoles. To this day, The Castro remains one of San Francisco's most colourful – and inclusive – neighbourhoods.

Streets of change
The Castro walk

Begin your walk atop the lovely ❶ *Corona Heights Park* for panoramic city views spanning the hilly Twin Peaks and the towers of the Financial District. This is also a good place to get your bearings of The Castro itself.

Walk south to exit the park on 16th and turn right onto Castro Street. As you cross Market Street you'll spot the famous neon sign of the Twin Peaks Tavern, one of The Castro's oldest gay bars, inscribed onto San Francisco's list of heritage sites in 2013. A few doors down is ❷ *Castro Coffee Company*, a neighbourhood institution owned by the Khoury family, which has been roasting its own coffee beans since 1986.

Continue south along Castro Street and stop outside the wedding cake of a building that is ❸ *The Castro Theatre*. Check the listings and get a ticket for the evening's show if you can – a singalong here is a quintessential Castro experience. One of the theatre's neighbours is the excellent ❹ *Dog Eared Books*, which opened in 1992. It specialises in books and magazines by independent publishing houses. Next, head south and take a brief detour onto 18th on the right to pop into the ❺ *GLBT History Museum*. Opened in 1985, it now boasts one of the most comprehensive archives of material relating to San Francisco's gay and lesbian communities.

When you're ready, return to Castro Street and turn right to reach venerated seafood joint ❻ *Anchor Oyster Bar*, which has been serving top-notch traditional fare such as clam chowder, fresh oysters and crab cakes since 1977. If seafood doesn't float your boat, take 18th east, turn left onto Noe Street and head north. At Market Street, veer right around the bank to ❼ *Starbelly* on the corner of 16th. This first-rate Californian comfort-food spot offers super-fresh salads, pizzas and sandwiches for lunch.

A little further east along 16th is ❽ *Eureka Valley/Harvey Milk Memorial Branch Library*. San Francisco's public-library network

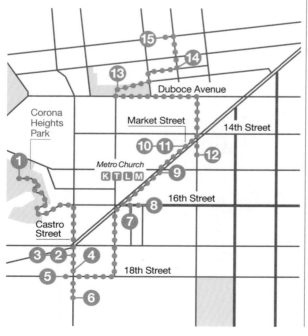

is one of the most used city library systems in the US and this branch was designed by city-based practice Appleton and Wolford in 1961, and renamed in memory of Harvey Milk in 1981.

Return to Market Street and walk right for another block. If you need to freshen up, stop for a trim at the no-frills **09** *Male Image* barbershop, which has been offering fresh cuts to The Castro's residents since 1979. Continue northeast along Market and, just before you hit Church Street, you'll find **10** *Lucky 13* on the opposite side of the road. During the 1960s and 1970s this former bar was abuzz with political activists. Next door is menswear spot **11** *Maas & Stacks*, carrying threads from the likes of Visvim and Our Legacy.

If you failed to treat yourself to something sweet at lunch, cross back over Market Street and head right on Church Street to visit the friendly **12** *Thorough Bread and*

Getting there

Bus number 37 leaves from right outside the Metro Church Station (serviced by Muni lines K, T, L and M) and drops you almost at the top of the Corona Heights Park hill, saving you the hike. Alternatively, stay on the metro to disembark at Castro and walk 15 minutes uphill.

Pastry bakery. If the weather's fine, take your pastry to go. Head north on Church Street, then left on Duboce Avenue to find a spot in **13** *Duboce Park*. This patch of greenery is a favourite among furry friends and their owners.

For the final stretch, leave the park at the northeastern edge and walk up Steiner Street. Turn right down Germania Street and then left on Fillmore Street to visit mixed retailer **14** *Revolver*, from the same talented team behind The Voyager shop (*see page 49*). There's just one final push uphill for two blocks, then turn left on Haight Street to pull up a stool at relaxed beer joint **15** *Toronado Pub* (*see page 43*).

Address book

01 Corona Heights Park
     Roosevelt Way & Museum
     Way, 94114
02 Castro Coffee Company
     427 Castro Street, 94114
     +1 888 528 2349
     castro-coffee.com
03 The Castro Theatre
     429 Castro Street, 94114
     +1 415 621 6120
     castrotheatre.com
04 Dog Eared Books
     489 Castro Street, 94114
     +1 415 658 7920
     dogearedbooks.com
05 GLBT History Museum
     4127 18th Street, 94114
     +1 415 621 1107
     glbthistory.org
06 Anchor Oyster Bar
     579 Castro Street, 94114
     +1 415 431 3990
     anchoroysterbar.com
07 Starbelly
     3583 16th Street, 94114
     +1 415 252 7500
     starbellysf.com
08 Eureka Valley/Harvey Milk
     Memorial Branch Library
     1 Jose Sarria Court, 94114
     +1 415 355 5616
     sfpl.org
09 Male Image
     2195 Market Street, 94114
     +1 415 621 6448
10 Lucky 13
     2140 Market Street, 94114
11 Maas & Stacks
     2128 Market Street, 94114
     +1 415 678 5629
     maasandstacks.com
12 Thorough Bread
     and Pastry
     248 Church Street, 94114
     *thoroughbreadandpastry.
     com*
13 Duboce Park
     Duboce Avenue & Scott
     Street, 94114
14 Revolver
     136 Fillmore Street, 94117
     revolversf.com
15 Toronado Pub
     547 Haight Street, 94117
     +1 415 863 2276
     toronado.com

Out of town
—— The best of
the Bay Area

01

If there's a problem with
the Bay Area, it's that
so much of it is worth
seeing. And while it's
hard to separate San
Francisco from the eight
other counties around
it, including them would
mean this book running
to several hundred pages.
   Still, it would be
remiss of us to ignore
the wealth of wonders on
offer in the surrounding
region. Here's a sampling
of places that are more
than worth the road trip,
from towering redwood
groves to headline-
making restaurants.

02   03

04

05   06

07

08   09

Address book

Point Reyes National Seashore, Marin County
Just 50km north of the city, this wild 28,700-hectare park has hikes, beaches, Native American sites and a lighthouse from 1870.
nps.gov/pore

Sir and Star at The Olema, Marin County
Incredible food (and value: try the $85 Saturday Night Supper) makes this farmhouse-style restaurant near Point Reyes well worth the drive.
sirandstar.com

Muir Woods, Marin County
This forest has been protected as a national monument for more than 100 years but the redwoods are 10 times that age and reach almost 80 metres.
nps.gov/muwo

Scribe Winery, Sonoma County
The picture-perfect scenery at this fourth-generation family winery almost makes you forget that you came to buy wine.
scribewinery.com

Berkeley Art Museum and Pacific Film Archive, Berkeley
The University of California's bright visual-arts hub hosts highly regarded screenings, exhibitions and performances.
bampfa.org

01   Point Reyes lighthouse
02   Point Reyes shipwreck
03   Cypress tree tunnel, Point Reyes
04   Marin County coastline
05–06 Muir Woods
07–08 Scribe Winery
09   Brothers Andrew (left) and Adam Mariani of Scribe Winery

01 02

03 04

01–02 Marin County
          Civic Center
    03 Katina and Kyle
          Connaughton of
          Single Thread
    04 Room at Single Thread
05–06 Oakland Museum
          of California
07–08 Paramount Theatre
09–10 Book/Shop

05 06

07

08   09

10

Address book

Marin County Civic Center, San Rafael
This landmark building, designed by Frank Lloyd Wright, has guided tours twice a week. If you can't make either, opt for the audio guide.
marincounty.org/depts/cu/tours

Single Thread, Sonoma County
All the ingredients for the Californian/Japanese dishes served at this fine-dining restaurant are sourced from its own farm. There's also an inn.
singlethreadfarms.com

Oakland Museum of California, Oakland
Combining history, art and natural science, the exhibits in this brutalist building are highly respected. Its Friday food-truck event is a tasty bonus.
museumca.org

Paramount Theatre, Oakland
Dating back to 1931, this cinema is a beautifully preserved example of art deco.
paramounttheatre.com

Book/Shop, Oakland
Lose yourself in Temescal Alley, a hive of local businesses from coffee shops to retailers, including this supplier of books, art and furniture.
shopbookshop.com

Best of the valley
Should you find yourself in Silicon Valley on business, your best bet is to stay in Palo Alto (The Clement Hotel has comfy rooms). Jin Sho, Evvia and Nobu are great for client dinners, while pizza joint Vesta is a good casual option. Plus, Tin Pot Creamery scoops up moreish classics.

Resources
—— Inside knowledge

Now that we've more or less filled your itinerary with places in which to eat, drink, shop and stay, we thought we would round it all off with a few helpful hints, including how to get from A to B, which events to plan your visit around and what to do come rain or shine. We've also thrown in some top tunes from the city and a bit of local lingo to boot.

Transport
Getting about

01 **Flights:** The San Francisco International Airport is about a 40-minute drive from the city centre. Ride-share companies respond quickly or the Bart rail service takes about 30 minutes for under $10. The Oakland International Airport is a 45-minute drive, while San Jose International Airport is best for Silicon Valley.

02 **Clipper Card:** Purchase and preload a Clipper Card to use the city's public transport services. To activate a journey, hold the card over a scanner and wait for the beep. Top up at Muni and Bart stations.
clippercard.com

03 **Muni Metro and buses:** Six light-rail lines service the outer neighbourhoods of Sunnydale, the Outer Sunset, Parkside, Oceanview, Portola Place and North Beach towards downtown, while an extensive bus network does the hard work for you on the hills.
sfmta.com

04 **Bart:** The tracks of the Bay Area Rapid Transport system service 21 cities and 400,000 commuters daily.
bart.gov

05 **Streetcars and cable cars:** Cable cars have been used here since 1873. Three routes still run, taking on the toughest climbs north of Market Street. The F Line (Fisherman's Wharf to The Castro district) still uses heritage streetcars.
sfmta.com

06 **Taxis:** Taxis may be hard to hail here but ride-sharing apps were born in San Francisco, so app-driven services are plentiful and reliable. Lyft is the carrier of choice for many.
lyft.com

07 **On foot:** While the Mission, Soma and the Financial District are fairly flat, it can get very steep north of the Tenderloin. Use the topography feature on your digital map for a better grasp of the landscape.

Vocabulary
Local lingo

01 **Karl:** the fog's nickname
02 **Hella:** used in place of "really" or "very" for emphasis
03 **Slaps:** great, catchy songs
04 **June gloom:** the inevitably cold, foggy summers
05 **415:** another name for the city, referencing its area code

Soundtrack to the city
Five top tunes

01 **Jefferson Airplane, 'Somebody to Love':** The city's reputation as a place of liberal values owes much to its position at the centre of the 1960s hippie counterculture. This classic from a local outfit was an anthem at the time.

02 **Sylvester, 'You Make Me Feel (Mighty Real)':** LA's Sylvester moved here as disco was taking hold in The Castro district in the early and mid-1970s. His hit is now one of the genre's touchstones and still fills dance floors today.

03 **The Units, 'High Pressure Days':** San Francisco synth-punk pioneers The Units embraced futuristic sounds in the late 1970s. This track is a jittery, tense masterpiece describing the feverish challenges of inner-city living.

04 **DJ Shadow, 'Organ Donor':** The Bay Area's hip-hop scene has influenced rappers from Tupac Shakur to Kreayshawn and Lil B. Resident DJ Shadow's 1996 classic album *Endtroducing* says much despite having hardly any vocals; obscure samples and beats do all the work.

05 **Thee Oh Sees, 'Contraption/ Soul Desert':** Psychedelia-inspired garage-rock bands have thrived in San Francisco – and none more so than Thee Oh Sees, led by frontman John Dwyer. But the city's increasingly pricey property boom has seen many artists like Dwyer moving on.

Best events
Get involved

01 SF Sketchfest, citywide: Both lauded and unknown names in comedy grace the city's stages for a full month. *January, sfsketchfest.com*

02 Chinese New Year Festival and Parade, Chinatown: The oldest Chinatown in North America puts on the largest Chinese New Year celebration outside Asia to celebrate the change in calendar. *January-February, sanfranciscochinatown.com*

03 Big Sur International Marathon, Big Sur: While not in San Francisco, this breathtaking marathon route sees runners tackle the roads that hug the rugged Pacific coastline. *April, bsim.org*

04 San Francisco International Film Festival, citywide: Perhaps overlooked, sitting in the shadow of LA's extravagant film celebrations, this two-week programme is deserving of attention. *April, sffilm.org*

05 Bay to Breakers, citywide: An annual fun run inaugurated in 1912, complete with crazy costumes – or birthday suits. *May, baytobreakers.com*

06 San Francisco Jazz Festival, SFJazz Center: This annual celebration of homegrown jazz musicians has been taking place for three decades and now occurs mainly in the SFJazz Center (*see page 93*). *June, sfjazz.org*

07 San Francisco Design Week, citywide: A comprehensive round-up of the Bay Area's creative talent that features their most outstanding examples of design. *June, sfdesignweek.org*

08 San Francisco Pride, citywide: A historic celebration of diversity and acceptance. Events occur across the city all weekend, with a colourful parade down Market Street on the Sunday. *June, sfpride.org*

09 San Francisco Fringe Festival, Tenderloin: About 40 companies from around the world perform their favourite but perhaps lesser-known shows at the Exit Theatre. *September, sffringe.org*

10 Folsom Street Fair, Mission District: Some 400,000 scantily clad leather and fetish enthusiasts gather for this. *September, folsomstreetevents.org*

Sunny day
The great outdoors

01 Soak in the views: Although beautiful in its own way, Karl the fog can really spoil the view. So when it's a clear day, head for the hills. Grandview Park requires a bit of a hike but from the top you can peer past Sutro Tower to downtown in the east or over the sleepy beachside neighbourhoods to the Pacific in the west. For a picnic, grab supplies from Dolores Park Café or Bi-Rite on 18th Street in the Mission, then head three blocks south to perch on the top of Dolores Park. The view down palm-lined Dolores Street is charming, so expect competition for the best spot.

02 Time travel: Alcatraz has had many historic incarnations: the first lighthouse on the West Coast; a Civil War fortress; a federal penitentiary; and the location of a political occupation known as the American Indian Red Power Movement. Head to Fisherman's Wharf early to beat the crowds and board one of the private boats to the island. Besides touring the historical landmarks, check out the stellar views back across the bay and the small pockets of nature. *nps.gov/alca*

03 Ball game: If it's baseball season and the sun is shining, head to AT&T Park to watch much-loved home team the Giants play a sunset game. Unlike most stadiums, the best seats here are the nosebleeds, with the horseshoe grandstand looking out over the pitch and onto the bay. Another major drawcard is the food, which isn't your average deep-freeze-to-deep-fryer fare: think fresh Dungeness crab on sourdough, organic fried-chicken sandwiches and Californian wines on tap.

Rainy day
Weather-proof activities

01 All aboard: Ride the classic streetcar F Line from start to finish. The route starts in The Castro district in the southwest, travels north to Fisherman's Wharf and passes landmarks such as The Castro Theatre, the Ferry Building and Pier 39. Get off at Jefferson & Taylor, walk three blocks west and board the Powell-Hyde cable car via Lombard Street, up and over Nob Hill and past Union Square.

02 Wine tasting: Tour California's best vineyards without leaving the city. William Cross Wine Merchants (*see page 40*) in Russian Hill is a top spot, while the Castro Village Wine Co has been a neighbourhood mainstay since 1978 and specialises in small-production wines. Hayes Valley outpost Arlequin Wine Merchant caters to a variety of budgets and the café next door is a good place for a pick-me-up. *wmcross.com; castrowine.com; arlequinwinemerchant.com*

03 Catch a play: As well as the usual companies (*see page 91*) there's Theatre Rhinoceros, the world's longest-running queer theatre. There's also the Exit Theatre, which has five in-house venues and looks after the San Francisco Fringe Festival, and the thought-provoking Brava Theatre Centre. *therhino.org; theexit.org; brava.org*

About Monocle
─── Step inside

London HQ
───
Our editorial
office is in
Marylebone

In 2007, Monocle was launched as a monthly magazine briefing on global affairs, business, culture, design and much more. We believed there was a globally minded audience of readers who were hungry for opportunities and experiences beyond their national borders.

Today Monocle is a complete media brand with print, audio and online elements – not to mention our expanding network of shops and cafés. Besides our London HQ we have six international bureaux in New York, Toronto, Singapore, Tokyo, Zürich and Hong Kong. We continue to grow and flourish and at our core is the simple belief that there will always be a place for a print brand that is committed to telling fresh stories and sending photographers on assignments. It's also a case of knowing that our success is all down to the readers, advertisers and collaborators who have supported us along the way.

1

International bureaux
Boots on the ground

We have a headquarters in London and call upon firsthand reports from our contributors in more than 35 cities around the world. We also have six international bureaux. For this travel guide, MONOCLE reporters Ed Stocker, Mikaela Aitken and Tomos Lewis decamped to San Francisco to explore all that it has to offer. They also called on the assistance of various writers in the city to ensure that we have covered the best in retail, food and drink, hospitality, entertainment and more. The aim is to make you, the reader, feel like a local when visiting Fog City.

2

Online
Digital delivery

We have a dynamic website: *monocle.com*. As well as being the place to hear our radio station, Monocle 24, the site presents our films, which are beautifully shot and edited by our in-house team and provide a fresh perspective on our stories. Check out the films celebrating the cities that make up our Travel Guide Series before you explore the rest of the site.

3

Retail and cafés
Food for thought

Via our shops in Hong Kong, Toronto, New York, Tokyo, London and Singapore we sell products that cater to our readers' tastes and are produced in collaboration with brands we believe in. We also have cafés in Tokyo and London. And if you are in the UK capital visit the Kioskafé in Paddington, which combines good coffee and great reads.

❹
Print
Committed to the page

MONOCLE is published 10 times
a year. We have stayed loyal to our
belief in quality print with two extra
seasonal publications: THE FORECAST,
packed with key insights into the
year ahead, and THE ESCAPIST, our
summer travel-minded magazine. To
sign up visit *monocle.com/subscribe*.
Since 2013 we have also been
publishing books, like this one,
in partnership with Gestalten.

❺
Radio
Sound approach

Monocle 24 is our round-the-clock
radio station that was launched in
2011. It delivers global news and
shows covering foreign affairs,
urbanism, business, culture, food
and drink, design and print media.
When you find yourself in San
Francisco tune in to *The Monocle
Daily* to hear regular reports from
our Toronto and New York bureaux
and interviews with guests from
across the Americas region. We also
have a playlist to accompany you
day and night, regularly assisted by
live band sessions that are hosted at
our Midori House HQ in London.
You can listen live or download any
of our shows from *monocle.com*,
iTunes or SoundCloud.

Priority service
———
Subscribers
save 10 per
cent in our
online shop

Join the club

01
Subscribe to Monocle
A subscription is a simple
way to make sure that
you never miss an issue
– and you'll enjoy many
additional benefits.

02
Be in the know
Our subscribers have
exclusive access to the
entire Monocle archive, and
priority access to selected
product collaborations, at
monocle.com.

03
Stay in the loop
Subscription copies are
delivered to your door at no
extra cost no matter where
you are in the world. We also
offer an auto-renewal service
to ensure that you never
miss an issue.

04
And there's more...
Subscribers benefit from a
10 per cent discount at all
Monocle shops, including
online, and receive exclusive
offers and invitations to
events around the world.

**Choose your
package**

Premium one year
12 × issues
+ Porter Sub Club bag

One year
12 × issues
+ Monocle Voyage tote bag

Six months
6 × issues

Chief photographer
Aaron Wojack

Still life
David Sykes

Photographer
Damien Maloney

Images
Alamy
Iwan Baan
Visit California
Mark Darley
Joe Fletcher
Douglas Friedman
Erik Heywood
Carol Highsmith
Drew Kelly
Charlie Lumanlan
Main County Civic Center
Jon McNeal
Shumai P
Andrew Pielage
Snøhetta
Jim Sommons

Illustrators
Satoshi Hashimoto
Ceylan Sahin
Tokuma

Writers
Mikaela Aitken
Barrett Austin
Erica Blume
Mallory Farrugia
Alastair Gee
Gary Kamiya
Tomos Lewis
Hugo Macdonald
Fabian Mayer
Blaine Merker
Nancy Pelosi
Mark Robinson
Elena Ruiz
Ben Rylan
Ed Stocker
Zoe Stricker
Bonnie Tsui

Monocle
EDITOR IN CHIEF AND CHAIRMAN
Tyler Brûlé
EDITOR
Andrew Tuck
CREATIVE DIRECTOR
Richard Spencer Powell

CHAPTER EDITING

Ⓜ
Need to know
Mikaela Aitken

Ⓗ ❶
Hotels
Ed Stocker

Ⓕ ❷
Food and drink
Mallory Farrugia

Ⓡ ❸
Retail
Mikaela Aitken

Ⓣ ❹
Things we'd buy
Mikaela Aitken

Ⓔ ❺
Essays
Ed Stocker

Ⓒ ❻
Culture
Tomos Lewis

Ⓓ ❼
Design and architecture
Ed Stocker

Ⓢ ❽
Sport and fitness
Tomos Lewis

Ⓦ ❾
Walks
Mikaela Aitken

Ⓞ ❿
Out of town
Mikaela Aitken

Ⓜ
Resources
Mikaela Aitken

**The Monocle Travel Guide
Series: San Francisco**
GUIDE EDITORS
Ed Stocker
Mikaela Aitken
ASSOCIATE GUIDE EDITOR
Tomos Lewis
PHOTO EDITOR
Victoria Cagol

**The Monocle Travel Guide
Series**
SERIES EDITOR
Joe Pickard
ASSOCIATE EDITOR
Chloë Ashby
ASSISTANT EDITOR
Mikaela Aitken
RESEARCHER
Melkon Charchoglyan
DESIGNER
Loï Xuan Ly
PHOTO EDITORS
Matthew Beaman
Victoria Cagol
Shin Miura

PRODUCTION
Jacqueline Deacon
Dan Poole
Rachel Kurzfield
Sean McGeady
Sonia Zhuravlyova

Research
Erica Blume
Beatrice Carmi
Melkon Charchoglyan
Elizabeth Cochrane
Audrey Fiodorenko
Edward Lawrenson
Charles McFarlane
Maïa S Heegaard
Paige Reynolds

Special thanks
Stewart Bean
John Bela
Mike Buhler
Paul Burditch
Melissa Buwembo
Lulu Cheng
James Enright
Natalie Enright
Melissa Farrar
Anthony Greenberg
Florie Hutchinson
Pete Kempshall
Anna Kuhn
Charleen Murphy
Lisa Petrie
Dana Polk
Olivia Rosen
Andrew Salzberg
Jeremy Schipper
Daniel Sherman
Zoe Stricker
Rob Thomson
Anthony Veerkamp

San Francisco
Index ———

The MONOCLE *Travel Guide Series* 22
Stockholm

The MONOCLE *Travel Guide Series* 23
Lisbon

The MONOCLE *Travel Guide Series* 24
Munich

The MONOCLE *Travel Guide Series* 25
Milan

New

The collection
Planning another trip? We have a global suite of guides, with many more set to be released in the coming months. Cities are fun. Let's explore.

Buy today at all good bookshops

You can also visit the online shops at *monocle.com* and *shop.gestalten.com* to get hold of your copies.

Right, where next?

- ❶ London
- ❷ New York
- ❸ Tokyo
- ❹ Hong Kong
- ❺ Madrid
- ❻ Bangkok
- ❼ Istanbul
- ❽ Miami
- ❾ Rio de Janeiro
- ❿ Paris
- ⓫ Singapore
- ⓬ Vienna
- ⓭ Sydney
- ⓮ Honolulu
- ⓯ Copenhagen
- ⓰ Los Angeles
- ⓱ Toronto
- ⓲ Berlin
- ⓳ Rome
- ⓴ Venice
- ㉑ Amsterdam
- ㉒ Stockholm
- ㉓ Lisbon
- ㉔ Munich
- ㉕ Milan
- ㉖ San Francisco